Optimizing AI in Higher Education: SUNY FACT² Guide, Second Edition

AUTHORS

Lynn Aaron, Rockland Community College

Santina Abbate, Stony Brook University

Nicola Marae Allain, Empire State University

Bridget Almas, SUNY System Administration

Brian Fallon, Fashion Institute of Technology

Dana Gavin, Dutchess Community College

C. (Barrett) Gordon, SUNY Erie

Margarete Jadamec, University at Buffalo

Adele Merlino, SUNY Maritime College

Laura Pierie, SUNY Morrisville

Gina Solano, SUNY Oneonta

David Wolf, SUNY Schenectady County Community College

Optimizing AI in Higher Education: SUNY FACT² Guide, Second Edition Copyright © by Faculty Advisory Council On Teaching and Technology (FACT²) is licensed under a [Creative Commons Attribution-NonCommercial 4.0 International License](#), except where otherwise noted.

eBook ISBN 979-8-8558-0183-5

Contents

Executive Summary ... ix

Foreword ... x

To The Reader ... xi
Billie Franchini and Jeffrey Riman

How to Use the Guide ... xi

Acknowledgements ... xii
Lynn Aaron and Dana Gavin

Part I. AI in Context

AI Meets the Public ... 2

A Year in AI ... 3

AI Capabilities ... 4

AI Bias Concerns ... 5

    Algorithmic Bias ... 5

    Data Management and Media Literacy ... 7

Societal Impact ... 10

    AI in Society: Ethical and Legal Issues ... 12

Intellectual Privacy Considerations ... 15

    Fair Use Vs. Copyright ... 15

    Licensing and Fair Compensation ... 15

    Impact On Trademark Infringement ... 15

AI Trademark Infringement ... 17

AI Literacy ... 18

    AI Literacy in Everyday Living ... 19

    Misinformation and Disinformation ... 22

Part II. Policy Considerations in Teaching and Education

Opportunities and Threats in Higher Education ... 25

    Equity and Access in Higher Education ... 26

Dealing with Academic Integrity … 28
    Integrity Problems with AI … 28
    False Honesty of AI … 28
    Psychological Impact of AI … 28
The Responsibility of Educators … 29
    The Impact of AI in Other Contexts … 30
    Information Security Concerns … 30
AI Policy Suggestions … 31
Additional Resources … 36

Part III. AI in Course Development and Assessment

Uses of AI Technologies in Higher Education … 38
    AI-powered personalized learning … 38
    Intelligent tutoring systems … 38
    Automated grading and assessment … 38
    Virtual and augmented reality … 38
    Intelligent content creation … 38
    Data analytics for educational insights … 39
    Language learning and translation … 39
    Intelligent learning management systems … 39
AI Capabilities for Students … 40
AI Tools for Student Writing Tasks … 41
AI Capabilities for Faculty … 42
Suggestions for Faculty AI Use … 43
Prompt Engineering for Instructors … 45
Setting Expectations in Your Classes … 46
AI Tools to Promote Student Learning and Success: Examples … 47
    In-Class Activities … 47
    Writing Assignments … 49
    AI Tools for Research Assignments … 51
    Lab Reports … 51
    Accessibility … 51
    Considerations for Online Classes … 52
AI Tools Can Support Teaching: Examples … 53

Part IV. AI in Student Research and Creative Works

The Role of AI in the Student's Research/Creation Process … 59

AI as it Pertains to the Intellectual Growth of the Student Researcher	60
Using AI to Develop Research and Scholarship	61
AI Literacy	61
Opportunities	61
Risks	61
Citing/Disclosing	62
Using AI to Evaluate Research and Scholarship	64
Funder and Publisher Guidelines	64
Using AI in Creative Works	65
Copyright, Intellectual Property and Applications in Creative Industries	66
Generative AI in Student Creative Works	67
Summary and Additional Considerations	67

Part V. Evaluating AI Tools in Higher Education

Student Evaluation Practices and Assessment Strategies	69
AI's Impact on Summative Assessment: An Example	69
Alternative Grading Strategies	71
Challenges with AI Detection Products	71
Strategies for Pedagogical Evaluation	73
Strategies for Technology Evaluation	74
Strategies for Accessibility and DEI Evaluation	76
Strategies for Student Input	77

Part VI. Special Section: A Brief History of AI

Part VII. Conclusion

What Does the Future with AI Look Like?	83
Job Market	83
Scientific Discovery	83
Cyber Security	83
AI and Mindreading	84
Interspecies Communication	84
After Death Communication (in a way)	85
Appendix A: Timeline	86

Appendix B: Algorithmic/Machine-Learning Bias	88
Machine Learning Bias	88
Examples of Algorithmic Bias	89
Appendix C: AI Tool Evaluation Examples	91
Example A: Midjourney	91
Example B: Almanack.ai	91
Example C: Learnt.ai	91
Appendix D: Glossary	92
References	96

Executive Summary

In late 2022, as ChatGPT emerged as a free and easily accessible tool that could generate text seemingly out of thin air, the education community was rocked. For some, this launch was anticipated, as this technology had been in development for decades. Many, however, were caught flat-footed and struggled to come to grips with not only what "generative AI" was, but how ubiquitous it was, how readily available it was to students, and the impact this "new" technology was going to have on many disciplines inside the academy.

In May 2023, the SUNY FACT^2 Task Group formed to create a guide as quickly as possible to address the issues as we understood them. The document offered an overview of the opportunities and challenges presented by generative AI, delivered pedagogical recommendations, and submitted a glossary and tool assessment compendium. Even as we were editing the final draft, we knew a revision would be necessary, as generative AI tools and applications were already developing quickly beyond the first iteration of the FACT^2 *Guide to Optimizing AI in Higher Education*. Reconvening quickly, we have endeavored to represent these evolutions and adaptations in the development of generative AI, while also sharing updates on ethical and legal concerns.

This document presents information and solutions to educators across the spectrum of enthusiasm and adoption interests, as we believe everyone should be empowered to make educated decisions for themselves and their students regarding generative AI. Perhaps the least effective response at this point is to pretend generative AI is not a part of the higher education experience. Thus, this document supports educators at all levels and disciplines; we are addressing the issue rather than engaging in avoidance.

In this *Optimizing AI in Higher Education: SUNY FACT^2 Guide, Second Edition*, you will find updated information to reflect the changing landscape of generative AI technology. We offer practical suggestions for how to help educators and students achieve AI literacy and find the right methods of using or eschewing generative AI in their pedagogy. The second edition represents both an update to the first *Guide*, but also a recognition of the fact that generative AI is a tool in constant development; we will continue to advocate for equitable education and access for all students and educators as this dynamic and innovative field continues to grow.

Foreword

As Provost Liaison to the SUNY Faculty Advisory Council on Teaching and Technology (FACT2), I am pleased to present this second edition of **Optimizing AI in Higher Education: SUNY FACT² Guide**, which was developed by the FACT2 Task Group on Optimizing Artificial Intelligence for Teaching and Learning. The first version of this *Guide* was developed in response to a call from the SUNY Provost in Spring 2023 to provide a guidance document for SUNY Faculty for the Fall 2023 semester, and it came together in record time over the summer of 2023. During the 2023-2024 academic year, the Task Group worked thoughtfully and carefully to expand the *Guide* to this second version, which was unveiled to the SUNY community at the SUNY Conference on Instruction and Technology in May 2024.

The quality of work represented in the pages to follow are a testament to the tireless efforts and dedication of the FACT² Task Group. Their invaluable work has culminated in this comprehensive resource designed to support faculty across the SUNY system in navigating the complex and rapidly evolving landscape of artificial intelligence in education.

The FACT² Council AI Task Group, comprised of faculty and staff from a range of SUNY institutions, as well as selected experts from outside of SUNY, spent a full year exploring the challenges and opportunities AI presents in higher education. Their collective expertise and truly collaborative spirit have enriched this second version of the *Guide* beyond what was originally envisioned, making it a vital tool for educators who are seeking to understand how AI can be used in the teaching and learning context, considering possible use cases, thinking through how they might integrate AI into their teaching practices responsibly and effectively, or evaluating specific AI tools. I am extremely grateful to the entire Task Group, especially those faculty and staff who worked over the Summer of 2023 to produce the first version of the *Guide*.

This *Guide* would not have been possible without the exceptional leadership of the FACT² Task Group Co-Chairs, Billie Franchini (SUNY Albany) and Jeffrey Riman (SUNY Fashion Institute of Technology). Their ability to steer the writing team and this *Guide* to completion was impressive, and I am grateful for their dedication to this publication. Additionally, their vision and clarity of purpose in leading the Task Group enabled the dedicated volunteers to produce a wide range of valuable resources and assets, beyond the *Guide*, to support SUNY faculty considering the use of AI in their classes.

The *Guide* was designed for SUNY faculty, but as we continue to witness the transformative impact of AI across all of higher education, this *Guide* serves as a crucial resource for faculty anywhere, providing insights, recommendations, and practical tools to enhance teaching and learning. We hope this work will empower educators to harness the potential of AI while recognizing the need to address the ethical, legal, and societal implications it brings.

Thank you to everyone involved for your hard work and dedication. You should all be proud of the *Guide* and are not only shaping the present but also paving the way for the future of AI in higher education.

Kim A. Scalzo

Interim Senior Associate Provost for Digital Innovation and Academic Services

SUNY System Administration

To The Reader

BILLIE FRANCHINI AND JEFFREY RIMAN

The FACT[2] Council on Optimizing Artificial Intelligence in Higher Education is very pleased to present the work of our subcommittee dedicated to updating and expanding the first edition of this *Guide*. This second edition was accomplished by a group of volunteers dedicated to teaching who explore the challenges and opportunities AI presents us. We understand that there are a lot of concerns and anxiety surrounding the inclusion of AI in the educational process. This *Guide* is designed to provide you with enough information to support you as you engage with this revolutionary change. We deeply appreciate the leadership of subcommittee co-chairs Lynn Aaron, Rockland Community College, and Dana Gavin, Dutchess County Community College and the contributions of all the subcommittee members listed on the Acknowledgements page that follows.

In addition to the *Guide*, our task group provides many other resources, including a YouTube channel with [recordings of our faculty development events](#) and our upcoming one-day [pre-conference symposium](#) on May 21 before the Conference on Instruction and Technology's (CIT) opening at the University of Buffalo. We hope to see you there.

How to Use the *Guide*

This *Guide* provides a comprehensive overview of AI in higher education and offers essential context for the development and use of AI tools. However, it does not have to be read beginning to end or in a specific order. In fact, because of its broad scope, some sections are not relevant to all teaching situations. We encourage you to identify the parts of the *Guide* that are most relevant for your context and read them in the order that makes the most sense to you.

Task Group Co-chairs:
Billie Franchini, SUNY Albany, and Jeffrey Riman SUNY FIT

Acknowledgements

LYNN AARON AND DANA GAVIN

We are delighted to recognize the colleagues who worked on this second edition of the *Optimizing AI in Higher Education: SUNY FACT² Guide*. Contributions have come from many sources.

First, we want to express our deep thanks to Billie Franchini (SUNY Albany) and Jeffrey Riman (SUNY Fashion Institute of Technology), FACT² AI Task Group Co-Chairs, for their thoughtful guidance and support. They have been there for us throughout the development of both editions of the *Guide* from start to finish.

We have had the pleasure of working together with colleagues who have expertise in distinct areas of the AI landscape. You – Santina Abbate (Stony Brook University); Nicola Marae Allain (Empire State University); Bridget Almas (SUNY System Administration); Brian Fallon (Fashion Institute of Technology); C. (Barrett) Gordon (SUNY Erie); Margarete Jadamec (University at Buffalo); Adele Merlino, (SUNY Maritime College); Laura Pierie (SUNY Morrisville); and Gina Solano (SUNY Oneonta) – have enabled us to expand the *Guide* into new areas while updating areas of growth. We further appreciate Nicola Marae Allain, Bridget Almas, Margarete Jadamec, Adele Merlino, and David Wolf, who, in addition, generously lent their skills to the overall review process.

Stephanie Pritchard (SUNY Oswego), we are grateful to you for volunteering your time and expertise to this project. You reviewed the manuscript in great detail and made numerous valuable suggestions and corrections despite not being an official member of the Guide Committee.

Bridget Almas (SUNY Administration), thank you for assuming the role of Web Committee Liaison which has evolved into shepherding the *Guide* into publication.

Natalie Leriche (SUNY Fashion Institute of Technology), thank you for the creation of the *Guide* cover and some other illustrations. The *Guide* benefits from your talent.

Finally, we would be remiss without acknowledging the contributions of all Task Group Committee Co-Chairs Meghanne Freivald (Alfred University), Ken Fujiuchi (Buffalo State University), John Kane (SUNY Oswego), Keith Landa (SUNY Administration and SUNY Purchase), and Stephanie Pritchard (SUNY Oswego) as well as of Brian Cepuran (D2L Labs) for their continuing support.

Guide Committee Co-Chairs

> *Lynn Aaron, SUNY Rockland Community College*
>
> *Dana Gavin, SUNY Dutchess Community College*

PART I
AI IN CONTEXT

AI Meets the Public

Artificial intelligence (AI), generally thought of as using computers to accomplish tasks requiring human intelligence, is not a new concept. However, generative AI, a type of AI system that can generate text, images, or other media in response to prompts, has suddenly become an omnipresent part of the academic scene. In the form of ChatGPT and others, generative AI hit campuses with a bang that could be heard around academia in late 2022. The chart seen here shows the record-breaking speed with which ChatGPT came into popular use (Hawley, 2023): it reached 1 million users in 5 days. Over the last several months, the academic community has watched and participated in the rapid progression and adoption of AI tools.

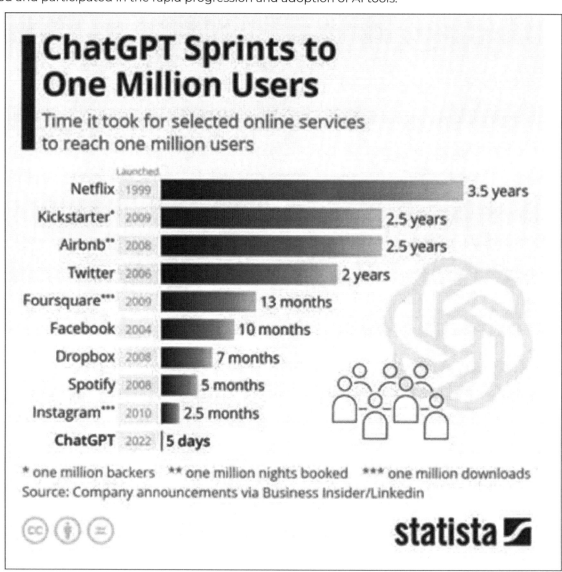

Speed of Generative AI Adoption

A Year in AI

Over the past year, progress in generative AI continued at an unprecedented rate (Perlow, 2023; Perrigo, 2023-a). Thanks to the progress of **Natural Language Processing (NLP)**, chatbot conversations have become more fluid as bots better understand language and provide quicker, more relevant responses (PM, 2023).

In addition, conversation with chatbots has become richer due to the development of **multimodality** (Perrigo, 2023-b). Originally (It's worth remembering we're talking weeks and months, not years), when we had a request, we provided text and got text responses. The use of voice for searching has now become popular, with fifty percent of mobile users using it regularly (Haan, 2023). A countless number of people have made asking Siri or Google Assistant a part of their everyday lives. ChatGPT (GPT-4) has advanced so it can now respond with voice (Metz et al., 2023).

More recently, the technology has advanced so that other modalities such as images and video can also be used to prompt a text response. This year, we saw that in OpenAI's GPT-4 and then in Google's Gemini. In a related development, it became possible to use text to generate images and even video. (Perrigo, 2023-c). Users can not only use text to have videos created, but also edit existing videos with text prompts.

Of course, the impact of this progress has been felt beyond the academic world. The growth of AI use in business has been notable. In a survey of the use of generative AI in corporations, one-third of those surveyed are using it regularly for at least one business function (McKinsey and Company, 2023). What was once a topic for IT departments only has reached management leadership, twenty-five percent of whom are using it for their jobs. They are also looking to the future. Forty percent plan to increase their investment in AI. Considerations of reskilling and reducing employees need to be addressed. There is work to be done and issues to resolve, but AI has landed in the corporate world.

So, too, has there been progress with values. Concern about inappropriate responses led to the development of something called "constitutional ai" (Mohan, 2023). A set of principles is developed, and bots are trained based on those, thus reducing the need for external human intervention and bias. The question, of course, remains about what values. Anthropic has made an effort to democratize this process by collecting values from a cross-section of the population (Perrigo, 2023-d). It is recognized as a step in the right direction, not a solution.

There's one other development this year that may broaden the impact of AI. Open source AI models are now available, allowing anyone to develop their own custom chatbots based on their own choice of data. Meta (Meta, 2024), for example, is currently offering a choice of open-source models focusing on different areas including language, reasoning, and computer vision.

We've come so far in a short period of time. People may be surprised to learn that AI actually started its evolution in the last century. For an understanding of how it developed over time, there is a new Special Section containing a brief history. The question now, for ourselves and our students — where will this take us?

AI Capabilities

AI capabilities involve the recognition of patterns in a set of data, which is processed by algorithms. These patterns can then be used to make predictions or create content. Many of us have interacted with AI through the use of Siri, Alexa, and recommendations from Netflix and other services (Calhoun, 2023). Our behavior online (and the data we provide through clicks and views) allows certain sites and applications to customize our experience, including the ads we see. A great deal of attention is being paid to generative AI, such as ChatGPT and similar tools. It uses conversational prompts (provided by users) to generate text-based information. It is important to note that ChatGPT and other Large Language Models (LLMs) do not engage in any actual "thinking." Rather, they are trained on large databases of information and have the ability to recognize patterns and to predict text (Shankland, 2023).

Likewise, LLMs are not capable of intent. Human communication relies upon our ability to interpret language as inherently conveying meaning and intent. But generative AI communication does not include intent on the part of the language model. As tools built on LLMs become increasingly fluent in using language to communicate, it becomes more difficult for human users of AI to remain aware that the interlocutor at the other end is just a machine that has been trained to predict the most likely words to use, and that any intent we assign to those communications is solely our own (Bender et al., 2021).

AI Bias Concerns

These applications necessitate that we consider how a variety of unsurfaced biases: -- language bias, culture bias, implicit bias -- can potentially affect the AI outputs we may obtain and utilize within these various departments (Ayling & Chapman, 2021; Hutson et al., 2022; Nguyen et al., 2023; Ungerer & Slade, 2022). Consequently, some of the previously mentioned concerns around data privacy and security, consent, accessibility, and labor and economy will be reflected in the microcosm of higher education (Irfan et al., 2023; Nguyen et al., 2023; Ungerer & Slade, 2022).

Algorithmic Bias

Algorithmic bias, sometimes referred to as machine learning bias or AI bias, describes when an algorithm systematically produces results demonstrating prejudice due to erroneous assumptions during the machine learning process. In general, there are two factors for the unfair outcomes: pre-existing bias that affects the machine/algorithms architectural design and bias resulting from the decisions relating to the training data, such as the way it is collected or coded for the training. While a program or machine may give the illusion of impartiality, in fact, the social and historical context surrounding the algorithm's design and decisions about the data used to train the algorithm have a direct result, either engineered or not, that may run contrary to our values on fairness.

Architecture Bias

While technically not a bias from machine learning, pre-existing bias can result in dissimilatory results that no amount of training data will correct. Design decisions that are influenced by pre-existing social biases implicitly create results unintended by the designers. For example, the TSA has been using full body scanners for over 15 years. The first scanners were designed with the strict, inflexible binary assumption about genders. The machines required an agent to select the gender before the scanning algorithm began (Hope, 2019). After the selection, training data would perfect detection of questionably dangerous objects on the subject. Regardless of the training data, the assumption about gender occurred from the first stage of development, and a machine that targeted the transgender population was the result. It was not until 2022 that the TSA began replacing these with gender-neutral scanners (Nyczepir, 2022). However, the algorithm's design was such that it ensured a biased result, and then poorly selected data input data was curated and used to confirm the bias in the design. Simply, the machines were designed with the assumption that there were only two distinct genders and training data ensured the machine would identify these. These biases may have been unintentional; however, the results were real.

Machine-Learning Bias

There are various ways machine-learning bias occurs due to the (mis)handling of data. Biases can manifest in various ways, but commonly reflect the data being used for training. Common to many forms of algorithmic bias are:

- The training data employs under-representative groups to be generalized as representative data
- Pre-existing prejudices are "pre-baked"' into the training data
- Interpretation bias from humans evaluating the output

An algorithm is only as good as it is designed, trained, and interpreted. Without careful controls, it can produce several undesirable results. A few types of machine learning bias include:

- Association bias
- Emergent bias (including feedback loops)
- Exclusion bias
- Language bias
- Marginalized bias (including; race bias, gender bias, sex bias, sexual orientation bias, disability bias, political affiliation bias, cultural bias, and colorism)
- Measurement bias
- Recall bias
- Sample bias

See Appendix B for more detail on the specific biases above.

While the number and variations of algorithmic bias seems vast, it does illustrate that the complexity of deep learning systems is not trivial and may exceed the ability of the people using them (Seaver, 2013). Knowing these biases occur is the first step in resolving the issue. Clearly there needs to be more scrutiny in data collection and its applications. Likewise, it demonstrates that context to data plays an important part in understanding the data. Finding spurious correlations may be entertaining, however their applications may result in direct discrimination (Goodman and Flaxman, 2017). In just a few years, AI systems have been deployed at a mass level and display algorithmic bias with devastating effects in areas such as hiring, healthcare, and banking. For detailed examples, see Appendix B.

Given the plethora of instances of algorithmic bias in AI, the decisions seem to be less a factor of intelligence and mostly just reflecting the bias that exists in our own world (Shah, 2018). Any of these cases would be considered a crime if a person came to the same decisions, given each unfairly targets legally protected groups. A problem occurs when this behavior arises from AI in that the algorithm is not a person, and frequently people will excuse the harm without accepting the seriousness of the damage. It is this phenomenon that makes AI bias particularly dangerous.

While artificial intelligence suggests that machines can mimic human intelligence, it is clear that these machines can also mimic undesirable biases as well. This is painfully clear with several generative AI systems. Simply observing image generation algorithms reveals a severe bias. Using Midjourney, Dall-E 2, and Stable Diffusion (three available AI image generation algorithms) yielded an insultingly stereotypical set of images. Out of thousands of images produced, a few cases illustrating algorithmic bias include:

- "An Indian person" would almost always produce an old man with a beard.
- "A Mexican person" was usually a man with a sombrero.
- "New Delhi streets" were polluted and littered in most every image (Turk, 2023)

Moreover, when countries are not specified in prompts, DALL-E 2 and Stable Diffusion generally use the United States or Canada as a default (Basu, Babu, and Pruthi, 2023).

Images for "An Indian Person" created by Midjourney

Above: out of 100 images created by Midjourney for "An Indian Person", most all were of an older bearded man wearing a headscarf or turban. India has over 1 billion people with approximately 80% being Hindu and only less than 2% Sikhs (that wear turbans). This set of outputs is not representative of the various groups of people from India. AI images from search by Turk, 2023.

Fixing the bias in AI generators will be a non-trivial problem. Part of what the algorithm (neural networks) do is identify patterns from data that they are trained on and frequently discard outputs that are not consistent with current trending outputs. This simply creates a feedback loop that reinforces the stereotype the algorithm identifies. Even when trying to avoid stereotyping by using more detailed prompts, does not correct the bias (Bianchi, 2023). For example, Stable Diffusion produced several image outputs of black persons when given the prompt "a poor white person". To make this problem worse, attempts to increase diversity to Google's image tool, Gemini AI, resulted in depicting a 1943 German soldier as either a black man or an Asian woman (Robertson, 2024). Google apologized for this, turned off Gemini's ability to generate images, and has yet to have solved the issue (Gilliard, 2024).

Data Management and Media Literacy

While AI often refers to "artificial intelligence," in many ways it is simply *automated intelligence*. It may seem fashionable to suggest that intelligence is emergent from the black box of a LLM, but this notion is dangerous and false. First, this allows companies to refuse to take responsibility for harm caused by carelessly creating biased models. Further, companies can rely on the 'impartial' or inscrutable algorithms, which creates a veil for companies to shield themselves from critical and moral examination (Martin, 2022). Even if algorithmic bias occurs through a corporation's ignorance, adhering to the algorithm without critically examining its reasoning subjects us to automated stupidity.

The claim that the algorithms are black boxes with emergent properties is misleading or, more likely, confessing to one's ignorance of how the algorithm works. Without knowledge of the data sets that train the algorithm, it becomes hard to describe its output. While AI can seem like magic, it is only data sets and knowledge about how the neural network operates. The outputs are not emergent. These properties vanish if users know what metrics to apply and use better statistics (Schaeffer, Miranda, and Koyejo, 2023). This is one reason why good data management is key for developing and understanding an algorithm.

Neural networks that implement a deep learning process can employ thousands of hidden layers or more. This can make it seem intractably difficult for humans to understand, however we do understand deep learning. Pre-training the AI models with data sets, which are often datasheets, is critical to this process. Understanding these data sets is vital for describing the model's behavior and eliminating algorithmic bias (Gebru et al., 2022). Moreover, given that correcting bias after the fact did not work well in the past, knowing the pre-training data for any LLM will vastly improve our ability to describe how the network is functioning (Yasaman et al., 2022). Being transparent about the data sets is key for determining algorithmic bias. We should note that OpenAI, the company that owns GPT-4, has yet to release their training data (Barr, 2023).

Better data management can reduce algorithmic bias and potentially reduce harming others by following simple rules. Munro (2019) suggested the following (well before the popularity of AI):

- Machine learning architectures should be developed by an iterative process combining human and machine components. Instead of using a black box approach, humans are 'in-the-loop' to assess progress during each step of the development.
- Basic annotation techniques should be applied when training data is being created. Understanding these ensures accuracy and efficiency in the annotations.
- Understanding key sampling techniques such as uncertainty sampling and diversity sampling will help strategize the right combination of approaches for particular problems.
- Understanding the causes of key algorithmic biases will avoid these mistakes in the algorithms

Each of these guidelines requires training and work. A company might not get this level of expertise from workers paid only $2 an hour, such as those from OpenAI (Perrigo, 2023).

The stakes for better data management are critically high. A Pew Survey (2018) revealed that 40% of Americans thought algorithms could acceptably evaluate job applicants. The acceptance of AI as an impartial tool is demonstrably false, as the evidence of algorithmic bias regularly appears in the news. More disturbing is that humans are inheriting the biases after using the AI tools (Vicente and Matute, 2023). Simply, by using the AI, they are absorbing and retaining biases. Since generative AI is already flattening concepts and promoting negative stereotypes, it stands to reason that these tools are perpetuating harmful biases.

Relying on corporations and data managers and regulations to resolve biases will not work at this stage of the game, as this will not be enough. One factor that can assist in tempering the adverse effects of algorithmic bias and how it influences humans is to make users more literate of the media and tools they are using. Media literacy of the public is a critical key for understanding and rejecting AI misinformation or bias created by bad actors, **hallucinations** from networks, or algorithmic bias. Currently, the level of information literacy in the US is poor, with a great increase in the number of people primarily getting news and information from social media (Newman et al., 2022). A Stanford study of 3,446 high school students suggested that teenagers lack the skills to reliably discern accurate online information (Breakston et al., 2021). Being influenced by algorithmic bias and misinformation from AI is only part of a bigger problem; the public needs more media literacy skills.

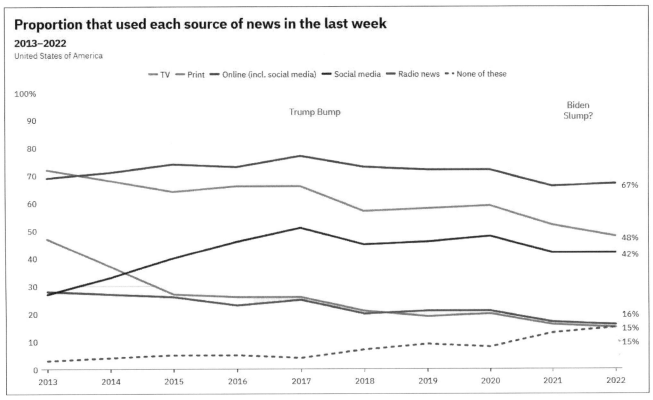

Comparison of news sources (2013-2022)

Investing in media literacy programs at all levels of education would combat the problem. In higher education, we cannot assume that learners will be entering with any media literacy training. Only two states, Delaware and New Jersey, have laws that mandate the inclusion of media literacy for K-12 students (Leedom, 2024) and there has been a steady decline in school librarians for years (Tomko and Pendharkar, 2023). Higher education needs to infuse media literacy throughout the curricula and demonstrate its commitment to it publicly. It is not enough to have students using AI tools, but they need to learn how to assess these tools and learn about their potential harm.

Societal Impact

When considering the current and potential social impacts of artificial intelligence, we should place the rise of artificial intelligence within the context of larger global shifts that are changing how humans live, communicate, work, and interact. These include climate change, global economic shifts, aging populations, migration, technological advances in areas such as AI, automation, biotechnology and renewable energy, social and political changes, and environmental degradation. These shifts have been exacerbated, and in some cases accelerated, by the recent Covid-19 pandemic and the changes this brought to social, economic, health, including mental health, and workplace experiences and environments (British Academy, 2021, Alizadeh et al., 2023).

According to the IMF report titled Gen-AI: *Artificial Intelligence and the Future of Work*, "Artificial intelligence (AI) is set to profoundly change the global economy, with some commentators seeing it as akin to a new industrial revolution. Its consequences for economies and societies remain hard to foresee" (Cassinga et al., 2024). Global society has experienced at least four industrial revolutions since the late 16th century, from mechanization to electrification, automation, and digitization (Groumpos, 2021). Each of these revolutions had a transformative effect on society and the world economy. In some cases, this was for the benefit of most common citizens. In others, workers were exploited and labored under dangerous conditions until unions formed and regulations were developed. Specific changes included urbanization and demographic shifts, changes in labor practices, wide-scale economic growth (often uneven, with growing disparities), and social changes, including changes in family structures and social norms.

Revolutions in communications technologies also had a radical impact on society. These included the telegraph, the telephone, radio, cinema, television, personal computing, the internet, and cellular communications (Kovarik, 2016). In our lifetime, many of us have experienced the rapid changes, positive and negative, incurred by the adoption of these new technologies in our professional and personal lives. The rise of artificial intelligence is usually placed in the broader category of changes we have seen since the 2000s that are a logical extension of automation and digitization within a world with the Internet of Things.

Given its wide reach into all aspects of 21st Century work and social interactions, areas for potential social impacts of artificial intelligence include the potential for significant influence on communication and relationships, employment and the economy, inequity and social structure, urban and rural population shifts, social and cultural norms as well as the potential to interfere with political discourse (Polyportis & Pahos, 2024). AI introduces complex ethical dilemmas, including privacy concerns, the potential for ubiquitous surveillance, the proliferation of biases, and problems that arise from potentially biased algorithmic decision-making. Existing concerns about data privacy, the digital divide, and growing disparities become even more pressing as we witness a wide-scale adoption of artificial intelligence tools across different fields.

The role of artificial intelligence (AI) in aiding the dissemination of false information, fake news, and fabricated images and videos is a topic of growing concern and complexity. AI technologies have the potential to both positively and negatively impact the information ecosystem. These have a role in spreading misinformation through the creation of convincing false content, including deepfakes, which are videos and audio recordings manipulated to make it appear as if individuals are saying or doing things they never did. AI can produce photorealistic images or write convincing fake news articles, blurring the line between fact and fiction (Kapoor & Narayanan, 2023). It could also automate the generation and dissemination of false information on a scale that was previously unimaginable. For example, AI tools could be used to create a multitude of fake accounts on social media platforms to instantly spread false information across networks. AI algorithms can analyze vast amounts of data to identify the most effective ways to disseminate false information to specific groups and amplify the impact of disinformation campaigns.

Recent research reports by leading organizations such as the International Monetary Fund, Goldman Sachs, and the Organisation for Economic Co-operation and Development (OECD) indicate that AI's impact on the labor market will be significant, with potential for both job displacement and creation. Goldman Sachs reported that 2 in 3 occupations could be partially automated by AI (Briggs & Kodnani 2023). According to the OECD Employment Outlook 2023, a key distinction of evolving artificial intelligence tools, including generative AI, is that it has the capacity to automate non-routine cognitive tasks such as information ordering, memorization, perceptual speed, and deductive reasoning. This extends the scope and reach of automation into white collar professions held by college graduates. The authors also note that while automation may replace routine jobs, new roles will arise as industry, education, and society transform in response to accompanying affordances and challenges. McNeilly and Smith (2023) note that "Whether the changes are good or ill for individual workers will depend on their occupation, firm, individual capabilities and ability to adapt. Some will adjust better than others. There will be winners and losers."

Artificial intelligence holds the promise of tremendous benefits to society, as long as its adoption is aligned with ethical frameworks and mitigation of potential misuse, whether unintentional or by design. In health care fields, for example, artificial intelligence is already improving diagnostic accuracy, patient care, and treatment personalization, and shows promise of providing more immediate access to health services. However, it also presents challenges related to data privacy, consent, and potential bias in treatment. While AI has the potential to significantly improve healthcare for the elderly, there's a risk of age-related biases in AI models if they are not trained on diverse age groups. There is also a risk of widening the gap in gender disparity in relation to working with artificial intelligence and the acquisition of AI fluency. To date, early AI adopters are overwhelmingly male, with the median AI user being male, aged 35-49 (FII 2024). Women are underrepresented in the field of AI development. In 2022, just one in four researchers who published academic papers on AI were female (Cairo, Lusso & Aranda, 2023). This impacts the types of AI technologies that are developed and can lead to gender biases in AI algorithms.

Existing AI systems already exhibit gender biases, typically reflecting biases in the training data. This could perpetuate stereotypes and discrimination in areas like hiring, healthcare, and finance. Goldman Sachs data indicates that "6 in 10 men vs. 8 in 10 women in the US workforce are exposed to generative AI replacing their jobs" (McNeilly & Smith, 2023). The same report predicts that 300 million jobs could be replaced by AI. On the flip side, in a report from the Organization for Economic Co-operation and Development, 63% of workers in finance and manufacturing agreed that AI improved job enjoyment, and 55% said that it improved mental health (OECD, 2023). It can be easier for people to talk to chatbots about mental health issues than HR personnel. Chatbots can help direct them to the most appropriate on-demand resources for their everyday stresses, or, for more serious issues, to therapists that best fit their needs (Cohen, 2023). The IMF report states that women and highly educated workers are consistently more exposed to, but also more likely to benefit from, AI (Cazziniga et al., 2024).

Other disparities include age and geographic distribution. Older generations may lag in their adoption of AI technologies, and the impact of AI on job automation may disproportionately affect older workers employed in fields replaced by new technologies. Older workers may be less adaptable and face additional barriers to mobility, as reflected in their lower likelihood of reemployment after termination. Historically, older workers have demonstrated less adaptability to technological advances; artificial intelligence may present a similar challenge for this demographic group (Cazziniga et al., 2024). There is already a significant disparity regarding access to AI technology between developed and developing countries. Less developed regions may lack the educational resources and infrastructure necessary for AI development and implementation. Wealthier countries are more likely to benefit economically from AI, which would exacerbate global inequalities. The impact of AI is also likely to differ significantly across countries at different levels of development or with different economic structures (Cazziniga et al., 2024, OECD 2023).

We can learn from historical industrial and technological disruptions to navigate the challenges and opportunities presented by AI. Higher education will benefit from taking a balanced approach that leverages AI's benefits while mitigating related risks, and ensuring equitable access to AI's advantages.

AI in Society: Ethical and Legal Issues

AI began to affect society and the employment landscape prior to the introduction of ChatGPT. Customer service chatbots and self-checkout have become commonplace. Some jobs, particularly in the customer service and manufacturing sectors, have been replaced by AI. Many resources, articles, and subject-matter experts assert that AI is a powerful tool that is not a passing fad. Generative AI will continue to impact employment and the economy. Experts suggest that AI will continue to take on specific tasks, but it will not fully take the place of workers (Hawley, 2023). There are many concerns that AI will replace human work and interaction. While AI can perform some tasks well, it is not perfect and cannot replace the human-to-human experience required by fields such as teaching and nursing.

Although AI may be used to replace task-based, entry-level jobs, new jobs will likely be created to design and manage it. Individuals and businesses must plan for the growth of AI and anticipate the ways in which they will be affected (Marr, 2023). From a higher education standpoint, this creates an opportunity to re-evaluate educational pathways in order to prepare students for a world in which AI is prevalent (Abdous, 2023). How can we prepare students to use AI effectively, and to have the skills required to work with and manage AI at a higher level?

Artificial intelligence has been used in one way or another in education for years. For example, search engines, personal assistants on phones, assistive technology to increase accessibility, and other technology all use some form of applied artificial intelligence. However, the recent widespread availability of generative Artificial Intelligence tools across higher education gives rise to ethical concerns for teaching and learning, research, and instructional delivery. Implicit bias and representation (Chopra, 2023), equitable access to AI technologies (Zeide, 2019), AI literacy education (Calhoun, 2023), copyright and fair use issues (De Vynck, 2023), academic integrity, authenticity, and fraud (Weiser & Schweber, 2023; Knight, 2022), environmental concerns (Ludvigsen, 2023; DeGeurin, 2023), and ensured development of students' cognitive abilities (UNESCO, 2022) all represent ethical challenges for higher education as AI integrates further into the curriculum, the classroom, and our work and personal lives.

Data sets play a critical role in machine learning and are necessary for any AI that uses an Artificial Neural Network (including what runs ChatGPT) to be trained. The characteristics of these sets can critically mold the AI's behavior. As such, it is vital to maintain transparency about these sets and to use sets that can promote ideals that we value, such as mitigating unwanted biases that may promote lack of representation, or other harms (Gebru et al., 2022). Biases have already been identified in AI systems used in healthcare (Adamson & Avery, 2018; Estreich, 2019) as well as in auto-captioning (Tatman, 2017). The EEOC, DOJ, CFPB, and the FTC issued a joint statement warning how the use of AI "has the potential to perpetuate unlawful bias, automate unlawful discrimination, and produce other harmful outcomes" (Chopra et al., 2023). The FTC is investigating OpenAI's potential misuse of people's private information in training their language models and violation of consumer protection laws (Zakrzewski, 2023). Industry leader Sam Altman, CEO of OpenAI (the developers of

ChatGPT), recently testified at a Senate hearing on artificial intelligence expressing both concerns and hopes for AI. He warned about the need to be alert regarding the 2024 elections, and he suggested several categories for our attention, including privacy, child safety, accuracy, cybersecurity, disinformation, and economic impacts (Altman 2023).

Furthermore, lawsuits have been filed alleging everything from violation of copyrights to data privacy to fair use issues (De Vynck, 2023). In addition to these legal challenges, labor concerns factor into this conversation as low-wage, uncontracted workers and labor from the global South have been used to train AI away from violent and disturbing content (Perrigo, 2023). Because AI is transforming labor and the economy through automation, higher education must respond to AI's potential to displace workers in many industries; we must teach our students the unique attributes and capabilities that humans bring to the labor market (Aoun, 2017).

Environmental factors add to the list of ethical concerns, especially in terms of energy and water consumption. For instance, ChatGPT uses as much electricity as 175,000 people (Ludvigsen, 2023) and the ChatGPT engine (GPT3) used 185,000 gallons (700,000 liters) of water to train. Each use of ChatGPT uses roughly a one-liter bottle of water (DeGeurin, 2023). In November 2022, New York became the first state to enact a temporary ban on crypto mining permits at fossil fuel plants (Ferré-Sadurní & Ashford). Academia must be cognizant of the environmental costs of generative AI.

UNESCO AI Ethics

AI ethics are a set of guiding or moral principles and techniques that help ensure the responsible development and use of artificial intelligence (AI). These principles are intended to ensure that AI is safe, secure, humane, and environmentally friendly, and that all stakeholders, such as engineers to government officials, use and develop AI responsibly.

Ethics Recommendations

Recommendations on the *Ethics of Artificial Intelligence* is a document adopted by UNESCO in November 2021. It provides a framework of values, principles, and actions to guide the responsible development and use of AI systems. The recommendation emphasizes the respect, protection, and promotion of human rights, human dignity, and the environment throughout the AI system life cycle. It highlights the importance of diversity, inclusiveness, fairness, transparency, accountability, and sustainability in AI governance. The document outlines policy areas such as ethical impact assessment, governance, data policy, international cooperation, and more. It aims to ensure that AI technologies work for the benefit of humanity while preventing harm and promoting peace, justice, and interconnectedness in societies (UNESCO, 2022, pp.7–22).

Transparency

Transparency plays a crucial role in AI systems by promoting accountability, trust, fairness, ethical considerations, legal compliance, public scrutiny, explainability, bias detection and mitigation, user empowerment, and regulatory compliance. It ensures that AI systems are accountable for their actions and decisions and builds trust between AI systems and users. In March 2024, the U.S. Department of Commerce (Goodman & United States Department of Commerce, 2024) concurred with the need for data transparency from AI tech companies. The government proposed that tech companies provide an "AI warning label" much like a nutrition label on food products, providing the details on how personal data is used to train AI models:

> Standardizing a baseline disclosure using artifacts like model and system cards, datasheets, and nutritional labels for AI systems can reduce the costs for all constituencies evaluating and assuring AI. As it did with food nutrition labels, the government may have a role in shaping standardized disclosure, whatever the form (Goodman & United States Department of Commerce, 2024, p. 71).

Transparency helps to address biases and discrimination, allows for ethical considerations, ensures compliance with legal frameworks, enables public scrutiny and oversight, facilitates the explainability of AI systems, empowers users, and ensures regulatory compliance (UNESCO, p. 22).

It is important to note that while AI technologies can greatly enhance education, according to the document on *AI Ethics Recommendation*, they should always be used in a way that respects and protects the rights and well-being of students. Privacy, data security, and algorithmic transparency should be carefully addressed for the responsible and ethical use of AI in education.

According to UNESCO (2022), stakeholders that should be involved in the monitoring and evaluation processes include:

- **Government** is responsible for developing and implementing legal and regulatory frameworks, as well as ensuring compliance with international law and human rights obligations.
- **Intergovernmental organizations**, such as the United Nations and its specialized agencies like UNESCO can provide guidance, facilitate cooperation, and promote the adoption of ethical standards at the international level.
- **The technical community**, including researchers, programmers, engineers, and data scientists have the expertise to assess the technical aspects of AI systems and identify any potential risks or biases.
- **Civil organizations**, including non-governmental organizations (NGOs) and advocacy groups can raise awareness, advocate for transparency and accountability, and ensure that the interests and rights of individuals and communities are protected.
- **Academia** and researchers can conduct independent research, provide expertise, and contribute to the development of ethical guidelines and best practices.
- **The media** can raise awareness, report on any potential risks or abuses, and hold AI actors accountable.
- **Policy-makers** at the national and international levels can develop policies and regulations, review the impact of AI systems, and make informed decisions based on the findings of monitoring and evaluation processes.
- **Private companies** have a responsibility to ensure that their AI systems are ethically implemented and to address any potential risks or biases.
- **Human rights and equality groups** can provide guidance, investigate complaints, and ensure that AI systems are compliant with human rights standards.
- **Youth and children's groups** are directly affected by the impact of AI technologies. Their perspectives and experiences should be considered to ensure that AI systems are inclusive and do not discriminate against or harm young people.

It is important to note that the involvement of these stakeholders should be inclusive and diverse in order to offer different perspectives, experiences, and interests. Collaboration and dialogue among these stakeholders are essential to ensure effective monitoring and evaluation of AI systems.

Intellectual Privacy Considerations

AI image generators can produce stunning watercolors, paintings, photos, and pencil drawings. Text generators are equally adept in creating poems, essays, mimicking styles while taking creative license in producing content that strays from facts (Appel et al., 2023). Consequently, the courts are trying to sort out how intellectual property (IP) laws pertaining to creative content should be applied to generative AI works of art.

Fair Use Vs. Copyright

AI and IP issues are currently being considered by US courts. Legal aspects of AI and IP include ownership and attribution, patentability, data privacy, and liability; laws and regulations such as copyright law, patent laws, data protection laws and international agreements and global standards for IP, will inform these legal aspects (Abdallah & Sallah, 2023). Abdallah and Sallah (2023) point to four ethical considerations for AI developers: transparency and accountability, bias mitigation, data privacy, and education/ ethical considerations.

Appel et al. (2023) highlight a case in late 2022, Andersen v. Stability, which involved three artists who sued multiple generative AI platforms on the basis that AI used their original, licensed work to train AI in their specific form and style, resulting in unauthorized plagiaristic art. The legal system is asked to clarify where the boundaries of plagiarism or "derivative works" have been crossed under IP laws. The question then becomes, does *Fair Use* allow copyrighted work to be used without the owner's permission for the intent of news reporting, teaching, scholarship, or research? Additionally, can such copyrighted content be utilized in a way that was not intended by the original creator?

Licensing and Fair Compensation

We must also consider licensing that provides compensation to the original artist who owns the IP and from the developers seeking to add the content to train AI tools. Until definitive rulings provide greater clarity and standards on IP in creative content using AI, it may be useful to focus on guiding principles that support ethical and responsible uses of AI. Holmes and Miao's (2023) UNESCO publication on *Guidance for Generative AI in Education and Research* states that, "While the emerging regulatory frameworks intend to require GenAI providers to recognize and protect the intellectual property of the owners of the content used by the model, it is becoming increasingly challenging to determine the ownership and originality of the overwhelming amount of generated works" (p. 36). The guide goes on to note "concerns about protecting the rights of creators and ensuring fair compensation for their intellectual contributions," and how the lack of traceability "introduces challenges into educational contexts about how the output of GenAI tools may responsibly be used" (Holmes & Miao, 2023, p. 36).

Impact On Trademark Infringement

Trademarks are recognizable signs, symbols, designs, or expressions that distinguish products or services of a particular source from those of others. Trademarks can be a word, phrase, symbol, or design, or a combination of these elements. They are used to identify and distinguish goods or services in the marketplace and can become valuable assets for businesses. Trademark laws govern the registration, protection, and enforcement of trademarks, ensuring that consumers are not confused about the source of goods or services.

AI Trademark Infringement

According to Zakir et al. (2023), AI impacts trademark law and raises several ethical issues pertaining to originality trademark infringement. AI-generated trademarks can potentially create logos, names, and other branding materials, which challenges the traditional understanding of trademark distinctiveness and originality. AI systems can analyze trends and design highly effective trademarks, which leads to an increase of AI-generated trademarks. AI's use of trademarks in online environments, typically used in digital marketing, raises issues of trademark infringement and dilution. AI systems can autonomously use existing trademarks, which may (and probably will) complicate the enforcement of trademark rights and the identification of infringement. Enforcing trademark rights in a digital landscape increasingly dominated by AI presents many challenges to current enforcement procedures that may need to be modified to address the identification of infringement generated by AI systems. This will require further systems and protocols to identify violation of trademark laws.

Zakir et al. (2023) suggest that AI-generated inventions could also raise questions about the eligibility criteria for patents. AI's involvement in the invention process also introduces the concept of whether AI can be recognized as an inventor. It ultimately questions how the standard legal concepts of novelty and non-obvious inventions apply to AI-generated inventions, as opposed to human inventions. Determining ownership of AI-generated trademarks and patents can be complex, as ownership rights come to the forefront when AI is involved in the creation process. This may involve considerations of the roles of the AI developer, the user, and potentially the AI itself. Liability issues may also arise when AI systems use existing trademark concepts.

At this point in time, the information provided in Zakir et al. is based on general knowledge of the impact of AI on intellectual property law and the potential implications for trademark law. The integration of AI into IP law raises ethical considerations including concerns about bias and fairness in AI systems as well as transparency and accountability in IP processes. Naturally, there are concerns that AI impacts human creativity. Balancing the promotion of innovation with the protection of IP rights in the era of AI requires careful ethical and legal considerations. These challenges highlight the need for adaptation and reform of IP laws, as well as patent laws to keep pace with technological advancements and ensure a fair and equitable IP ecosystem in an increasingly AI-driven world.

Zaker et al. encourage international cooperation and collaboration to develop harmonized standards and approaches to AI and IP law. Due to the global nature of AI technology and its impact on IP rights, it is important for different jurisdictions to work together to establish consistent and cohesive regulations that can effectively address the challenges posed by AI. Developing ethical guidelines and principles for the use of AI in IP, according to Zakir et al., could involve establishing ethical frameworks that address issues such as bias, fairness, transparency, and accountability in AI systems used in IP processes. These guidelines would help ensure that AI is used in a responsible and ethical manner, protecting the rights of human creators and promoting fairness in IP-related decisions. Also, implementing compulsory licensing structures for AI-generated works could provide a way to use these works while ensuring fair compensation to rights holders. Guidelines are essential in achieving a balance between encouraging innovation and creativity, while ensuring that the benefits of AI-generated works are available to all. Equally important is the promotion of education and awareness among policymakers, legal practitioners, and the general public regarding AI and its impact on intellectual property rights. This would help ensure that stakeholders have a comprehensive understanding of the challenges and opportunities presented by AI in the context of IP, enabling them to make informed decisions and develop effective policies.

AI Literacy

Preparing Students for the Future: Teaching AI Literacy

As AI tools and models become increasingly available, students will likely be expected to make use of them in a range of academic and professional settings. AI will also likely become a core part of common tools, with the line between non-AI and AI features becoming increasingly blurred. Faculty can develop courses to help students build the digital literacy skills that will be required to engage technology of every kind. In-class and independent assignments can guide students to master (and think critically about) prompt engineering, as well as the quality of the content that AI tools generate.

Laupichler et al., (2023) describe AI literacy as: "the ability to understand, use, monitor, and critically reflect on AI applications without necessarily being able to develop AI models themselves." This definition suggests that all students, in any discipline, would do well to understand:

- the historical context of generative AI;
- the current ethical debates surrounding generative AI;
- the current applications of generative AI in various disciplines and industries;
- and critical frameworks that help assess AI tools and applications.

Educators aiming for AI literacy should touch on each of these areas, though they may choose to dive into one or more of the areas with more detail. At minimum, students who possess AI literacy will understand that generative AI is not a new invention, be able to describe some main ethical (and legal) challenges surrounding the technology, identify a few of ways AI is being deployed in their field, and demonstrate the ability to use this knowledge to evaluate AI tools and applications.

Depending on the focus and scope of their class, the educator could offer a summary of numbers 1-3, or they could dive into explicit lessons and discussions on each topic. Some educators might wish to refrain from having their students use generative AI as part of their coursework, but that does not mean the students cannot become fluent in the language and function of generative AI as we understand it today. They can touch upon or explore the long history of generative AI as it has progressed from ELIZA to Copilot, for example, and have students debate ethical usage in different settings. Students should leave their courses with, at minimum, a brief understanding of what generative AI is and how it is used in the discipline/field, regardless of how they practically apply it within the course.

The University of Florida has developed an "AI Across the Curriculum" initiative to provide all students the opportunity to develop their AI skills for future workforce participation. This will be accomplished through a combination of foundational courses, including "Fundamentals of AI" and "Ethics, Data, and Technology". They're also offering disciplinary courses such as:

- "AI in Agricultural and Life Sciences"
- "AI in Social Sciences"
- "AI in the Built Environment"
- "AI in Media and Society"

This means students have the ability to earn a certificate in AI to complement their degree. This approach does have the downside of requiring adding on several stand-alone courses to a student's degree. However, consideration of the learning outcomes identified in the University of Florida's program or other similar models might help institutions or programs find opportunities to infuse AI across the curriculum in existing courses

However, even without AI directly integrated into the curriculum, there are already some resources that are available to students. For example, the University of Sydney has created a great website called AI in Education, which is a guide for students (created by students!) with information like creating resumes, understanding content, and overcoming writer's block. There will certainly be more information like this for students in the future, which is one of the reasons it's so important to be transparent about these tools now.

Case Study: AI in Design

One example of a field that has already seen the impact of AI is the field of design, which is rapidly evolving. While generative AI tools such as Midjourney and DALL-E (AI that generates images from prompts) have only begun to grab the attention of the general public recently, AI design tools have been used in the industry for some time. For example, Midjourney, Netflix's AVA (aesthetic visual analysis) is a collection of tools and algorithms which encapsulate the key intersections of computer vision combined with the core principles of filmmaking and photo editing. This AI is being used to create the thumbnails and trailers based on users' interactions with the content on the platform. Similarly, Alibaba's AI tool, Luban, is capable of creating eight thousand customized banner ads in one second. Even before the hype AI is currently receiving, many everyday interactions were created by a small design team using AI tools (or, in many cases, created *entirely* by AI).

In addition, AI is being used to automate many tasks that were traditionally done by designers, such as generating layouts, creating color schemes, and even coming up with new ideas. Here are three examples of different AI tools in design and what they can do:

- Adobe Photoshop's Content-Aware Fill uses AI technology to select and blend the best replacement pixels.
- Adobe Firefly uses generative AI to create many kinds of free art.
- Figma's AI Designer plugin can streamline and enhance the user experience design process.
- Topaz Gigapixel AI can upscale and enhance image detail and resolution by 600%.

Now designers have more flexibility to tackle even more important tasks beyond design production. AI will not replace designers, but it will change the role of designers in the future. Designers will need to bring creativity, critical thinking, and problem-solving skills to the creative process, but they will also need to be proficient with AI tools and technologies.

AI Literacy in Everyday Living

An important component of AI literacy is awareness of the multiple ways AI is impacting the lives of students today — both within and beyond their college education. This is important to us as well, and not only as educators. AI is quickly becoming pervasive.

There have already been significant AI contributions in such disparate fields as arts and entertainment, climate change, cybersecurity, disabilities, healthcare, infrastructure, jobs, mental health, politics, and more. Examples can be a powerful aid to understanding. These areas are likely to continue to be foci of AI growth, though the specifics will grow over time:

Climate Change

With its abilities to classify and predict, AI is used in many ways that involve climate change. It has been used to predict future trends, forecast global temperature changes, and anticipate phenomena such as El Niño (Cowls et al.). It should be noted there are also concerns regarding the carbon impact of AI development and usage on our environment (Keller et al., 2024).

Smartphone use

AI is making a difference in our use of smartphones in many ways. In addition to voice assistants (e.g., Siri, Google Assistant), it improves photography by responding to the environment (such as low light) provides real-time language translations, and more (Qualcomm Technologies, Inc., n.d.).

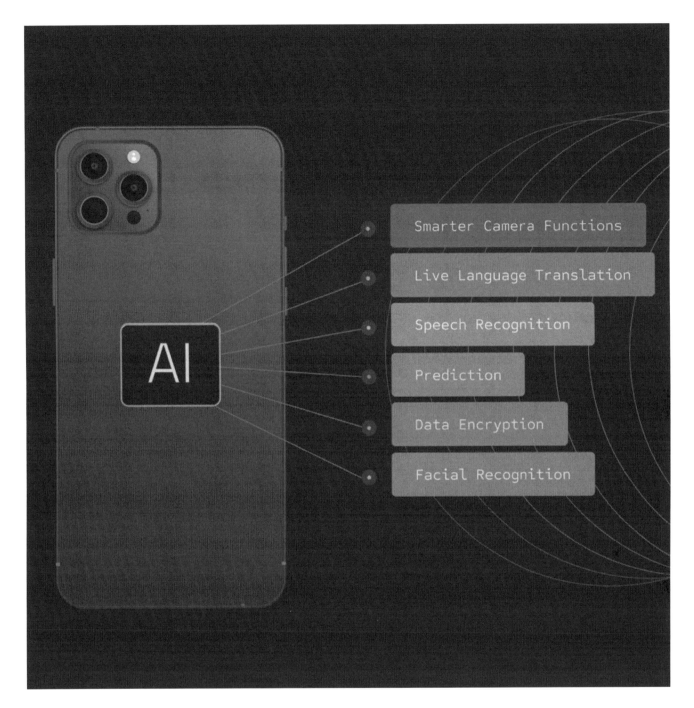

AI Uses in Smartphones

Mental Health

AI has made contributions to several aspects of mental health. Chatbots have been found to play a role, particularly in areas such as depression and anxiety. Woebot, developed at Stanford University, is such a bot with responses limited to recognized treatment approaches such as Cognitive Behavioral Therapy (Woebot Health, 2024). Findings support the suggestion that patients can form bonds with these conversational agents and show improvement (Darcy A et al., 2021).

They may even have particular benefits for college students (Maples et al., 2024) and the elderly (Valtolina, Stefano & Hu, Liliana, 2021). Bots can help to provide companionship, reminders, and general support.

Other studies looked at the diagnosis of psychiatric disorders. AI can be useful in their prediction, diagnosis, treatment, and monitoring (Terra et al., 2023). For example, AI's analysis techniques contribute to the value of MRI results as well as of EEG signals used in the diagnosis of psychiatric disorders (guang-Di et al., n.d.). With its growing abilities, AI can be, and is likely to become increasingly, useful in the recognition of emotions, improvement of communication during treatment, identification of high risk of suicide, and prediction of remission after treatment, among others (Terra et al., 2023).

Shopping

Our online shopping experience is now shaped by AI in several ways. It helps personalize our shopping experience and make it more efficient. For example, an Amazon order can now go from being placed to readied for delivery in 11 minutes (Van Cleave, & Novak, 2023).

Healthcare

AI's contributions go well beyond mental health. It has quickly become a vital part of our healthcare system (Pandey, 2024). From early detection through AI's image recognition skills, to improved diagnostics through its ability to quickly analyze massive amounts of data, to precision in robotic surgery, the improvements in healthcare have been felt throughout the field.

Entertainment

Streaming services like Netflix provide recommendations about what users would like to view next by analyzing behavior and previous choices. AI is also involved in other ways, for example optimizing streaming by determining how best to encode the video so as to maximize quality while minimizing file size (Kjandelwal et al., 2033).

Everything mentioned here is likely to become obsolete soon, replaced by even more powerful contributions to our lives. As we have discovered, unfortunately, there's another side to it.

Misinformation and Disinformation

Clearly there are benefits to artificial intelligence, but its pitfalls can be deep. Deepfakes are now part of our culture and are becoming increasingly realistic. We've already seen them in several areas ranging from misinformation in entertainment such as the Tom Cruise deepfake you may have seen (Inspired Learning, 2022) and the Jordan Peele video of Barack Obama to *dis*information in politics such as the Joe Biden robocall (Bushard, 2024; Satariano & Mozur, 2023; Vincent, 2018).

How will we deal with this? Will technology ultimately provide a solution to the problem it has created? A difficult question confronts us as educators (and human beings) — how do we learn, and teach, when to *not* trust our eyes? It may be that technology will offer solutions, but in an area with such rapid development, it's unlikely those solutions will remain effective over time. How do we unlearn a habit we've been using throughout our lives? That social experiment is underway.

PART II
POLICY CONSIDERATIONS IN TEACHING AND EDUCATION

Opportunities and Threats in Higher Education

There are many opportunities and threats related to generative AI, and both must be weighed as we move forward with policy development. Given the magnitude and variable nature of AI, there will not likely be a one-size-fits-all solution to the application and adaptation of generative AI in higher education instruction (Piscia et al., 2023). However, there are still many important points to consider concerning generative AI.

It seems impossible and inadvisable to not consider the interoperability of ethics and equity across domains of higher education (Currie, 2023; Hutson et al., 2022; Nguyen et al., 2023). One cannot underestimate the significance of privacy, security, safety, surveillance, or accountability whatsoever. The integration of AI into medicine and healthcare, financial systems, security systems, and smart city technologies represent very real-world situations in which machine malfunction or bad actors can result in loss of life, access to essential services, or loss of resources (Ayling & Chapman, 2022; Currie, 2023). However, many of the challenges surrounding higher education involve barriers to equitable access and educational services and resources. Therefore, any way in which AI may undermine equity should be treated as a significant ethical concern. It is worth noting, however, that AI also has the potential to improve or enhance accessibility and inclusivity (Çerasi & Balcioğlu, 2023). AI also has the potential to enhance teaching and learning (du Boulay, 2022; Perkins, 2023; Sabzalieva & Valentini, 2023; Sullivan et al., 2023) in ways that can improve or increase equity, which suggests that perhaps higher education has an obligation to integrate AI into its operations as much from an equity and ethics perspective as it does an experiential learning/workforce development or industry obligation to adequately prepare its students for real world work.

In considering the ethics of AI in higher education, it may be most useful to approach this situation through different stakeholder groups, namely students, instructors, and the institutions themselves (du Boulay, 2022; Holmes et al., 2023; Irfan et al., 2023; Miron et al., 2023; Ungerer & Slade, 2022), as well as through external groups such as industry collaborators and the communities in which those institutions operate. Within the institution, as noted above, AI has the potential to affect non-academic elements which cannot be ignored. Furthermore, the impact on the educational elements can vary in terms of programs, disciplines, and modalities, such as in-person instruction versus distance-based education (Holmes et al., 2023). Some researchers have expressed concern around how AI may or can compromise the autonomy of both students and instructors (du Boulay, 2022).

What does this all mean for educators? If we are to believe the experts as well as our own recent experiences, many issues need to be addressed. The current version of artificial intelligence seems to be just the beginning. The emergence of AI has been described as the dawn of a new era, a virtual big bang if you will. That is the world for which our students need to be prepared.

It is important to acknowledge and consider the positive aspects of the learner's experience regarding the use of generative AI in higher education. In many cases, generative AI may improve the experiences of our students both in the classroom and in their assigned work by introducing new methods of teaching and assessment (Piscia et al., 2023). As learners experience these tools in the classroom, students are learning and strengthening skills for their future endeavors and new realities within the classroom and in the workforce.

The inclusion of current and up-and-coming technology is imperative in education in the same way it drives progress and change in society. Fluency with generative AI tools will increase digital literacy and technology application for learners (Piscia et al., 2023). Additionally, students may be drawn to the inclusion of this tool in instruction, increasing the sense of relevancy of classwork and participation for students (Piscia et al., 2023).

The application of generative AI by instructors can also strengthen instruction, personalize learning opportunities, increase adaptability of instruction and learning, and strengthen accessibility for all learners (Piscia et al., 2023 and Shonubi, 2023). Each of these opportunities together increases inclusion in the classroom for all learners. AI tools can also be applied to the creation and/or modification of instructional objectives, pedagogy, and assignments and assessments.

Further, generative AI can be used to automate administrative tasks to improve workflows, decrease human transcription errors, and decrease processing times in many areas. Additionally, the application of generative AI in this way has the potential to decrease administrative costs and streamline administrative tasks (Parasuraman & Manzey, 2010, Piscia et al., 2023, and Shonubi, 2023). Generative AI has significant potential across a variety of higher education settings; instructional and learning environments in particular.

Additionally, institutions could be preparing students now for professions that are reduced or eliminated by generative AI presence in the workforce in the future. And the human aspect of interacting with generative AI must be not only considered, but studied as we move forward with this new tool at our disposal (Piscia et al., 2023 and Shonubi, 2023).

Congruently, it is imperative to consider the negative aspects of generative AI as well. The current lack of regulation and inconsistent accuracy of output are shortcomings that cannot be ignored. Generative AI is an evolving tool that needs to be carefully considered prior to its use.

Equity and Access in Higher Education

As indicated above, equity is crucial. Equity and access concerns for AI in higher education include fairness in outcomes across demographic groups, strategizing to identify and curb biases, and ensuring inclusivity and accessibility in the utilization of AI tools. Traditionally marginalized, underrepresented, and vulnerable groups must be consulted to ensure their experiences are represented in the datasets that drive AI and to limit AI from amplifying historical inequities (Munn, 2022, p. 874). Institutions of higher education must safeguard data privacy and protect against reinforcement of existing inequities. According to Roshanaei et al. (2023), this involves protecting sensitive student data, transparency and consent, strong data protection measures, and new regulatory frameworks. They draw attention to three risks to equitable AI integration in educational settings: biases in AI algorithms, the digital divide, and undermining the role of teachers (Roshanaei et al., 2023). Systems of higher education have an obligation to close the digital gap for students from low-income backgrounds who might not have access to reliable wifi, not to mention more advanced AI educational and assistive technologies only available behind a paywall.

Furthermore, the teaching and learning relationship must retain a human touch (Holmes & Miao 2023; Nguyen et al., 2023; Roshanaei et al., 2023). AI in education should function as an assistive tool and should not be used in place of teachers, tutors, mentors, counselors, or advisors. Holmes and Miao's (2023) UNESCO publication *Guidance for Generative AI in Education and Research* underscores the danger of generative AI to undermine human agency. One of its recommendations is to, "Prevent the use of GenAI where it would deprive learners of opportunities to develop cognitive abilities and social skills through observations of the real world, empirical practices such as experiments, discussions with other humans, and independent logical reasoning" (Holmes & Miao, 2023, p. 25). According to the same report, use of these tools have unknown impacts on human connection, human intellectual development and psychological factors for learners. Maintaining humanistic principles and involving people in the decision-making process is necessary to ensure fair representation and equal access in both the development and use of AI technologies for education (Nguyen et al., 2023; Munn, 2022).

Although AI poses risks to equity and access, it also has the potential to enhance and increase equity by supporting student success through personalized learning support and analytics to aid student persistence and achievement. Roshanaei et al. (2023) describe how personalized learning systems can offer targeted learning experiences tailored to various learning styles and paces. For instance, personalized learning systems can foster educational equity by providing assistive technologies for visual and hearing impairments, engaging and adaptive learning

environments, and analytics geared toward interventions for at-risk students. Of course, data privacy remains a concern, especially when using predictive analytics, but some benefits to predictive analytics might include identifying students' strengths and weaknesses, potential risks of dropout or failing, and developing interventions uniquely designed to get individual students back on track (Rashanaei et al., 2023).

Any use of AI tools must foster inclusion, equity, cultural and linguistic diversity and provide access regardless of gender, ethnicity, special educational needs, socio-economic status, geographic location, displacement status and any other barrier to equitable opportunities for learning. Holmes and Miao's (2023) UNESCO publication *Guidance for Generative AI In Education and Research* highlights three policy measures to reach this goal:

- Identify those who do not have or cannot afford internet connectivity or data, and take action to promote universal connectivity and digital competencies in order to reduce the barriers to equitable and inclusive access to AI applications. Establish sustainable funding mechanisms for the development and provision of AI-enabled tools for learners who have disabilities or special needs. Promote the use of GenAI to support lifelong learners of all ages, locations, and backgrounds.
- Develop criteria for the validation of GenAI systems to ensure that there is no gender bias, discrimination against marginalized groups, or hate speech embedded in data or algorithms.

Develop and implement inclusive specifications for GenAI systems and implement institutional measures to protect linguistic and cultural diversities when deploying GenAI in education and research at scale. Relevant specifications should require providers of GenAI to include data in multiple languages, especially local or indigenous languages, in the training of GPT models to improve GenAI's ability to respond to and generate multilingual text. Specifications and institutional measures should strictly prevent AI providers from any intentional or unintentional removal of minority languages or discrimination against speakers of indigenous languages, and require providers to stop systems promoting dominant languages or cultural norms. (p. 24)

Dealing with Academic Integrity

The growing concerns for academic integrity have created the immediate need for educators to adapt to new teaching practices. This change is to ensure AI supports the learning process without reducing students' cognitive abilities and preserving their access to prerequisite skills and the social aspects of teacher-student and peer learning relationships (UNESCO, 2022). In addition to concerns regarding cheating and fraud, there are also valid concerns about the reliability of AI-generated results and their potential to exhibit bias.

Integrity Problems with AI

ChatGPT has already been documented to fabricate information and adamantly defend these fabrications (Knight, 2022). Often these cases are referred to as hallucinations, as the chatbot produces responses as though they are correct. It is estimated that ChatGPT produces approximately 4.5 billion words a day (Vincent, 2021). This flow of content has the potential to degrade the quality of information that is available from the internet. There is no way at this point for AI tools to authenticate the content it retrieves, which suggests using caution when choosing an AI tool or trusting the outputted information.

False Honesty of AI

Kidd and Birhane (2023) argue that repeated exposure to AI (in daily life, like chatbots and search engines) conditions people to believe in the efficacy and "honesty" of AI. They contend that AI's method of using declarative statements without expressions, nuance, and caveat continues the process of convincing people to "trust" the AI. The use of unmonitored AI tools may result in a decline of critical thinking and may negatively impact content area learning, retention, writing development, creativity, and application (Miller, 2023). The burden of creativity and validity, therefore, lies with the humans who use AI to do their thinking instead of themselves.

Psychological Impact of AI

Artificial Intelligence is rich in potential but cannot be counted on to be accurate or representative. Both of these are of concern for our students. We do not want students to believe and/or use misinformation, and we do not want the information presented to them to be based on misleading data. There's also a potential mental health concern that arises when dealing with chatbots. Chatbots have come closer to sounding as if they are human, which can have a psychological impact on students as they build relationships with bots that may not respond humanely and with the student's best interest in mind (D'Agostino, 2023).

Interacting with generative AI tools may increase anxiety, addiction, social isolation, depression, and paranoia (Piscia et al., 2023). Although the studies of the impact of interacting with AI systems are in progress and shaping our understanding of the potential impacts of the tool on individuals and on society, a deeper, more complete understanding is yet to come and will develop in the coming years.

The Responsibility of Educators

AI is going to present teachers with incredible opportunities, but they will have to consider carefully how they are teaching and assessing students now that free platforms like ChatGPT are widely available. While AI can serve as a tool to help both teachers and students learn, it can not replace what is often the best part about higher education: the discussion, critical thinking, and mentorship that occurs in and out of a classroom. There is a history of tools that initially seemed threatening to education, but were later incorporated into instruction (e.g., calculators, Wikipedia, etc), and faculty would be well-served by approaching generative AI in a similar manner (Hicks, 2023).

While there is still debate about the extent that generative AI will transform education (Marcus, 2023; NeJame et al., 2023; Office of Educational Technology, 2023), faculty will need to encourage students to learn how to balance the information they get from AI with their own perspectives or creative expressions. Students will need to learn how to use these tools because they might be required to master them in their jobs when they graduate. However, it is important to stress that using artificial intelligence is not the same as thinking, which is why this technology should not control curriculum or content. Instead, faculty should set expectations and policies about the use of AI so students have clear guidance.

Despite the challenges for academic integrity and student learning, students will need to use these tools and educators have an obligation to instruct them on AI literacy, ethics, and awareness. Part of higher education's obligation in this regard is that we can include disciplines outside of the STEM fields to research and contribute to our knowledge of AI development and capabilities (UNESCO, 2022).

In a recent discussion among faculty on this topic, Nicola Marae Allain, Dean of the School of Liberal Arts and Humanities at Empire State University, looked further into the future. "So these tools are here now. They're only going to get better, more complex, more ubiquitous, present, and available."

We have a responsibility to our students to help them understand artificial intelligence, she points out. But we also have a responsibility "to think carefully about: How should it be used? Where should it be used? How could it be used? What do students need to know to use AI effectively in their fields?"

It's also worth mentioning that AI tools can be incredibly helpful for faculty and staff – these changes don't just affect our students. We can use this technology to create examples, quizzes, sample essays, in-class activities, discussion questions, study guides, or other resources for students. AI can be used for plagiarism detection, research assistance, or help give feedback on student work. However, just because you can use it doesn't mean you always should. Chapter 3 of this document provides additional detail on some considerations to keep in mind when deciding if and when to use AI.

The World Economic Forum (Partovi & Hongpradit, 2024) posits 7 principles for using AI in education:

- Purpose: Connect the use of AI to explicit educational goals.
- Compliance: Ensure that the use of AI supports institutional policies.
- Knowledge: Teach proper skills when using AI.
- Balance: Understanding the risks associated with AI and not overusing it.
- Integrity: Promote ethical use of AI.
- Agency: Human decision-making must be on the forefront.
- Evaluation: Regularly review the role and impact of AI.

The Impact of AI in Other Contexts

While it is critical to consider the ethical impact of AI like ChatGPT on academic integrity and academic dishonesty, there are other aspects of higher education that will be impacted that have ethical components. AI has been integrated into processes in human resources, financial aid, the student experience, diversity, equity, inclusion and belonging (DEIB), and institutional effectiveness. In many cases, AI integration in these domains is meant to enhance decision-making and assist in data analysis (du Boulay, 2022; Holmes et al., 2023; Naik et al., 2022; Nguyen et al., 2023). One must also consider the ethical impacts of integrating AI into educational platforms, like expert systems, intelligent tutors/agents, or personalized learning systems/environments (PLS/E), and teaching and learning perspectives (du Boulay, 2022; Hutson et al., 2022; Ungerer & Slade, 2022). Students and educators need to be aware of the type and content they are feeding into the AI tool, especially because the more it's used, the more data it gathers.

Information Security Concerns

Information security is a crucial factor to consider when adopting generative AI tools (Piscia et al., 2023). It is important to evaluate the information required to use generative AI tools, the confidentiality of completed queries and potential for data hacking. Additionally, data sharing between the tool and private entities must also be evaluated.

AI Policy Suggestions

The following table is a sample of how colleges and universities in the United States present their stance on the use of artificial intelligence. A common concept noted is academic freedom. Higher education promotes the autonomy of its instructors to teach in the manner they see fit. It is important to note that academic freedom has its limits that defer to the general laws of society (Britannica, 2024). In terms of AI, instructors have the latitude to determine where their course sits on the continuum of prohibition and permission. The majority of schools offer sample syllabi statements to guide faculty in communicating the rules and regulation of AI use to students.

Another commonality is that the use of AI without permission is considered a breach of academic integrity and is subjected to disciplinary action. The current state of AI is that it remains virtually undetectable, and schools generally discourage the use of AI detection applications due to the high prevalence of false positives. Therefore, this caveat (limitation?) is the main source of complexity and begs the question, how can an instructor prohibit the use of AI when there is no definitive way to discover its use within an assignment?

Statements that expressly prohibit the use of AI seem to be untenable at this time and may induce fear that could impair the integrity of the instructor-student relationship. Arousing alarm does not change the reality that AI remains indiscernible, therefore, statements prohibiting it are neither viable nor recommended. Instead, best practices are evolving to guide instructors to move away from prohibition until AI detection programs become a reliable way to detect its use.

Sources for AI-related Syllabus Statements

Institution	Type	Excerpts & Notes	Link to full policy/statement
SUNY Binghamton	Website Statement from Center for Learning and Teaching	Offers sample syllabi statements for prohibition or permission of AI use. *The use of generative AI tools or apps for assignments in this course, including tools like ChatGPT and other AI writing or coding assistants, is prohibited.*	SUNY Binghamton Generative Artificial Intelligence in Higher Education
SUNY Buffalo	Website Statement to students from the University at Buffalo	*UB has no single rule about using AI. Every instructor has the academic freedom to decide if/when these technologies are permissible in their class. Please consult them and/or your syllabus, and never assume that it is allowed. If your professor doesn't say anything, don't use it.*	University at Buffalo Artificial Intelligence (the other AI)
SUNY Geneseo	Website Statement from the Teaching and Learning Center	Offers sample syllabi statements for prohibition or permission of AI use. *Any work written, developed, or created, in whole or in part, by generative artificial intelligence (AI) is considered plagiarism and will not be tolerated.*	Geneseo Resources on Generative AI in the Classroom

SUNY Oneonta	Website Statement from Faculty Center for Teaching, Learning and Scholarship	Offers sample syllabi statements for prohibition or permission of AI use. *Please prepare and submit your own original work for this course. Do not use generative AI tools to complete any portion of an assignment or examination. Any use of AI tools will be considered plagiarism.*	SUNY Oneonta Faculty Resources: AI Syllabus Policy Examples
SUNY Potsdam	Website Statement from College Library	Views plagiarism and ChatGPT as a sliding scale and is explained in ChatGPT, Chatbots and Artificial Intelligence in Education.	Potsdam AI & Plagiarism
SUNY Suffolk	Website Statement on Academic Misconduct	Use of AI is listed as an example of plagiarism. *Using material generated by artificial intelligence tools for an assignment without instructor authorization.*	Suffolk County Community College Academic Misconduct Definitions
SUNY Stony Brook	Academic Integrity Policy for Division of Undergraduate Education	Use of AI is listed as an example of academic dishonesty. *Representing work generated by artificial intelligence as one's own work.*	Stony Brook University Academic Integrity Policy/

Cornell University	Website Statement by Center for Teaching Innovation	Offers sample syllabi statements for prohibition or permission of AI use. *To ensure development and mastery of the foundational concepts and skills in this course, the use of generative artificial intelligence (AI) tools is prohibited…please know that appropriate and ethical use of generative AI tools will likely be a part of other courses in your academic program.*	Cornell University AI & Academic Integrity
Harvard University	Statement located on Information Technology website	Initial guidelines written by the Provost and Executive leadership: *The University supports responsible experimentation with generative AI tools, but there are important considerations to keep in mind when using these tools, including information security and data privacy, compliance, copyright, and academic integrity.*	Harvard University Initial guidelines for using ChatGPT and other generative AI tools at Harvard

The Ohio State	Website statement by Office of Academic Affairs	*To maintain a culture of integrity and respect, these generative AI tools should not be used in the completion of course assignments unless an instructor for a given course specifically authorizes their use… these tools should be used only with the explicit and clear permission of each individual instructor, and then only in the ways allowed by the instructor.*	The Ohio State University Artificial intelligence and academic integrity
University of Pennsylvania	Website statement by Center for Excellence in Teaching, Learning and Innovation	Offers sample syllabi statements for prohibition or permission of AI use. *Faculty can completely forbid students from using it or they can allow certain uses (like using AI to help revise a draft or to generate topics.)*	UPenn Academic Integrity Statements that Address Generative AI/

When formulating syllabus statements faculty might want to consider the practicality of prohibiting AI use. While our first instinct might be to ask students to avoid using it, that's not practical. As Margarete Jadamec of the University at Buffalo points out, "We should be cognizant of whether or not objective standards exist to assess it." At this point, the answer would have to be "not"; they do not (yet) exist. David Wolf goes further, "With the growing technological advances, it would be unwise to try to prohibit it" (SUNY Schenectady County Community College).

The SUNY FACT[2] Task Group on Optimizing AI in Higher Education offered a webinar in March 2024 on **Developing Syllabus Statements on AI Use**. The presenters, Meghanne Freivald, Alfred University, and Keith Landa, SUNY Purchase and SUNY System Administration, offered this Syllabus Statement Template, which may serve as a starting point for faculty developing their own syllabus statements.

AI Policy Suggestions | 35

Additional Resources

Instructional Designers may also wish to consult **10 Ways Artificial Intelligence Is Transforming Instructional Design** for specific uses relevant to their needs including Personal Learning, Adaptive Learning, Intelligent Tutoring Systems, Natural Language Processing, and Gamification, among others.

Other institutions are exploring the impact of AI in education. One useful resource is Cornell University's [CU Committee Report: Generative Artificial Intelligence for Education and Pedagogy](#) which offers concrete examples of AI usage and policies.

PART III
AI IN COURSE DEVELOPMENT AND ASSESSMENT

Uses of AI Technologies in Higher Education

AI technologies can be used in education to support learning in several key ways:

AI-powered personalized learning

AI can analyze student data and provide personalized recommendations and feedback to students, helping them to learn at their own pace and in their own style. This can enhance student engagement and motivation, as well as improve learning outcomes.

Intelligent tutoring systems

AI can be used to develop intelligent tutoring systems that provide individualized instruction and support to students. These systems can adapt to the student's needs, provide immediate feedback, and offer additional resources and explanations when necessary.

Automated grading and assessment

AI can automate the grading and assessment process, saving instructors time and providing students with timely feedback. AI algorithms can analyze student responses and provide accurate and consistent grading, allowing teachers to focus on providing targeted instruction and support.

Virtual and augmented reality

AI technologies can be integrated with virtual and augmented reality tools to create immersive learning experiences. This can help students visualize complex concepts, explore virtual environments, and engage in interactive simulations, enhancing their understanding and retention of knowledge.

Intelligent content creation

AI can assist in the creation of educational content by generating personalized learning materials, adaptive textbooks, and interactive multimedia resources. This can help teachers customize their instruction and provide students with engaging and relevant learning materials.

Data analytics for educational insights

AI can analyze large amounts of educational data to identify patterns, trends, and insights that can inform instructional practices and educational policies. This can help educators make data-informed decisions and improve the effectiveness of teaching and learning.

Language learning and translation

AI-powered language learning platforms can provide personalized language instruction, speech recognition, and translation services. This can support language acquisition and communication skills development for students learning a language.

Intelligent learning management systems

AI can enhance learning management systems by providing intelligent recommendations for course selection, study plans, and learning resources. This can help students navigate their educational journey more effectively and efficiently.

AI Capabilities for Students

Many institutions of higher education are scrambling to both mitigate challenges ChatGPT can bring, like plagiarism, while simultaneously trying to harness its capabilities for student learning. As ChatGPT has become widely available, it is clear that students have begun experimenting with it and similar tools. In a professional development workshop given in the spring of 2023 at SUNY Morrisville, Kira Brady and Laura Pierie delivered a presentation titled "What Does AI Look Like in Your Discipline? The Changing Landscape of Higher Education." In the presentation, Kira identified markers of essays written by ChatGPT, and she also spoke to how lengthy the process can be to provide evidence that an essay was written by ChatGPT.

An opinion piece from the *Chronicle of Higher Education* provided this quote from a student, "I'm a student. You have no idea how much we are using ChatGPT. No professor or software could ever pick up on it." The author concludes that institutions must teach students to use AI, as it is a tool which is helpful and readily available. The author also suggests that faculty incorporate assignments that truly assess and promote skill development, including those which incorporate the use of AI tools (Terry, 2023).

How can professors help students harness the power of ChatGPT and other AI tools? As an example, Laura Pierie (SUNY Morrisville) has encouraged her students to use generative AI for writing resumes and cover letters in a professional writing class. Students completed a cover letter and resume without the help of AI, and then used ChatGPT. The class discussed whether the changes helped their resume and cover letter, and why or why not. During this process, they were able to utilize their voice, employ scientific reasoning, and demonstrate their understanding of the technology. Uses of AI tools are going to continue to evolve and grow. When considering these uses, it's important also to remember the limitations of AI and LLMs and the associated risks.

AI Tools for Student Writing Tasks

AI tools are dramatically changing the way that students and professionals write. These tools can be leveraged to save time, improve the quality of one's writing, check for missing citations, and thus result in a better-finished draft. While AI can be used to write in place of the author, it can also be used to monitor writing to develop better sentences, check for grammar and punctuation errors, and help paraphrase large pieces of text.

The recommendation for using AI writing tools is to have it boost our creativity instead of replacing it. While AI can be used to brainstorm ideas, it's important that the idea be chosen and developed with the human user's creativity and ingenuity.

Here is a list of recommended AI writing tools that do a variety of jobs without necessarily doing all of the thinking:

- Grammarly
- Citation machine
- myEssai
- LanguagePro
- Perplexity.ai
- Jenni.ai
- Semantic.ai
- GPTionary
- ProWritingAid

AI Capabilities for Faculty

AI has the potential to support faculty during the teaching process. Simulated students can be created by AI language models. Faculty can seek real-time feedback from generative AI, as well as post-teaching feedback. AI can provide metrics on student participation and identify faculty-initiated questions which provoked the most engagement during class. Faculty may also use AI to remain updated in their fields and create curricula (Chen, 2023).

Generative AI tools, particularly ChatGPT, may be used to speed up time-consuming tasks that educators perform routinely, such as updating unit outlines, lesson plans, and drafting prompts for writing or discussion. Instructors can also generate materials such as assignment instructions, flash cards, posters, rubrics, and assessment materials (Finley, 2023).

The Learning Management System Brightspace will be offering enhanced AI features for all users.

- The Brightspace Virtual Assistant is an AI-based help tool that is integrated directly into the learning environment. This chat assistant allows users to surface information, resources, and how-to guides as users need, right when they need them.
- Advanced tools auto-generate captions for videos and audio clips in Brightspace in multiple languages. Users can record, upload, and edit captioned video content from almost anywhere in the platform.
- The Adaptive Learning tool in Performance+ automatically builds an understanding of student progress against objectives, then links concepts to content to create unique learning paths for each student.
- Predictive Analytics in Performance+ compares key learning and engagement factors to identify patterns or risk factors so educators can take corrective action sooner.
- The Generative AI Beta program offers a suite of AI-powered enhancements to everyday workflows, including generating practice questions, generating quiz questions, and inspiring ideas for assignments and discussions. All enhancements are based on existing course content.

If educators understand the pros and cons of generative AI writ large and want to use generative AI in their classrooms, the following section gives practical applications for types of activities and their implementation in classrooms and for online classes.

Suggestions for Faculty AI Use

AI technology potentially offers students a more personalized approach to learning and creates the opportunity for instructors to be more innovative in their approaches to curriculum design while enhancing student motivation and autonomy (Alqahtani et al., 2023). The significant advances in AI are intrinsically linked to the future of higher education and best pedagogical teaching practices. While the initial response of educators might be to prevent the students' use of AI tools such as ChatGPT, the desperate attempt of finding a solution capable of detecting AI-generated text in student assignments has proven futile. Proving plagiarism via a detection technology can be considered inclusive evidence at best, as a viable solution does not yet exist. The implications can already be seen and signals a wave of change in higher education. This paradigm shift points to an adjustment to how instructors approach teaching and learning. The following are suggestions for AI best practices in the classroom:

Providing Clear Expectations. In the course syllabi and within the classroom, instructors must clearly articulate their expectations of students' use of AI in academic assignments. This entails that:

- instructors explicitly state in each assignment whether the use of AI tools is permissible or not. This transparency ensures that students understand the boundaries and guidelines surrounding AI usage in their coursework.

- instructors should consider providing a list of recommended AI tools that students may utilize for their academic tasks. This can serve as a helpful resource, guiding students towards reputable and effective AI tools while also minimizing the potential for misuse or unethical behavior.

Model AI Use. Instructors play a crucial role in modeling ethical AI use to their students. By demonstrating responsible and transparent engagement with AI technologies, instructors can instill a culture of integrity and respect for academic standards.

Additionally, to foster a supportive learning environment,

- **Create low-stakes assessments.** Instructors may choose to allow the use of AI tools on smaller stakes assignments. This provides students with opportunities to familiarize themselves with AI applications in a low-risk setting, promoting experimentation and skill development.

- **Replace some written assignments with projects.** In addition to traditional written assignments, instructors may opt to incorporate project-based assessments that leverage AI technologies. This approach not only diversifies assessment methods but also encourages creativity, critical thinking, and collaboration among students.

- **Compare student writing with AI-generated text.** To safeguard academic integrity, instructors can implement various strategies, such as testing assignment prompts against AI-generated content to identify discrepancies in writing skills. If suspicions of AI usage arise, instructors should engage in open and constructive conversations with the students involved, allowing them to clarify their actions and understand the ethical implications.

- **Discussion with the university's intellectual integrity committee or legal department.** In cases where the instructor's assignment guidelines are violated and the use of AI cannot be conclusively proven, instructors may seek guidance from other university support structures to assess the situation and determine appropriate courses of action.

Prompt Engineering for Instructors

According to Amatriain (2024), prompt engineering in generative AI models is a rapidly emerging discipline that shapes the interactions and outputs of these models. Prompt engineering is the practice of designing and refining prompts to elicit specific or desired responses from AI models such as ChatGPT. It can be thought of as the interface between "human intent and machine output" (Crabtree, 2024). The value of learning to engineer prompts for instructors will be to design and implement instructional prompts that guide students' attention, cognition, and actions towards the desired learning outcomes. These prompts are strategically crafted to stimulate engagement, promote deeper understanding, and facilitate effective learning processes. Additionally, prompt engineering is a powerful instructional strategy that can enhance learning outcomes, foster critical thinking, promote active engagement, support differentiated instruction, and ensure alignment with learning objectives. By leveraging well-designed prompts, instructors can create effective learning experiences that empower students to achieve academic success.

Enhance Learning. Well-designed prompts can streamline the learning process by directing students' focus towards critical information or tasks. By presenting clear and concise instructions or questions, prompt engineering helps students navigate through complex material more efficiently.

Critical Thinking Skills. Contrary to the idea that AI use can diminish critical thinking skills, learning prompts can stimulate higher-order thinking skills such as analysis, synthesis, and evaluation. By posing thought-provoking questions or problem-solving tasks, instructors encourage learners to engage in reflective thinking and explore diverse perspectives. This can cultivate a deeper understanding of the subject and promote intellectual growth.

Promoting Active Engagement. Prompt engineering can prompt students to actively participate in their own learning process rather than passively consuming information. Creating prompts, such as discussion prompts or collaborative activities, can encourage peer interaction, knowledge sharing, and collaborative problem-solving. This active engagement can foster a sense of ownership over the learning process.

Supporting Diverse Learners. Learning prompt engineering allows instructors to tailor instructional prompts to meet students' diverse needs and preferences. By providing multiple prompts or offering choice-based prompts, instructors can accommodate various learning styles, interests, and skill levels. This promotes personalized learning experiences and enhances learner motivation and engagement.

Ensuring alignment with Learning Objectives. Learning prompt engineering should be closely aligned with the course's intended learning outcomes and instructional goals. Prompts should be designed to scaffold learners' progression toward mastery of specific concepts, skills, or competencies. By maintaining alignment with learning objectives, instructors ensure that prompts effectively support learning and assessment practices.

Setting Expectations in Your Classes

It is essential to be transparent with students when it comes to using AI, including when the educator is using generative AI to draft educational materials. Faculty should choose carefully the extent to which they adopt AI in the coming year. Several institutions of higher education have developed policy statements. Faculty who are interested in suggestions for theirs can check the [AI Policy Suggestions](#) section in Chapter 2 of this *Guide*.

Setting clear guidelines will be essential to maintaining a fair and constructive learning environment. When faculty clearly define their expectations (at the beginning of the semester and as it progresses) students will begin to understand how to use AI tools responsibly, ethically, and appropriately. We should continually emphasize the value of critical thinking – to encourage our students to use AI as a resource instead of as a substitute for independent thought.

A syllabus statement can be as broad or specific as you wish. This statement provided by Shyam Sharma (SUNY Stony Brook) discusses the goals of using AI in the course, standards of academic integrity, the acceptable uses of AI, and how it should be cited:

Representing work generated by artificial intelligence as one's own work is academically dishonest. This class uses AI tools to reinforce your learning, using this approach:

1. Learn to use AI tools skillfully, as benefit increases with user skills;
2. Cross-check AI tools responses, even factual, against authentic sources, evaluating them carefully;
3. Cite all instances of words / ideas borrowed from AI tools using the MLA style;
4. For purposes beyond the cited text / ideas, indicate what AI tools you used and how in an endnote;
5. Don't use AI tools when not appropriate such as for logical or ethical reasons.

AI Tools to Promote Student Learning and Success: Examples

This section offers a variety of examples of how AI tools can offer valuable learning opportunities in both the humanities and in STEM, including in-class activities and sample assignments that can be used across the disciplines. It also considers accessibility and how AI tools like speech recognition or closed captioning can help diverse learners. These developments are not fully inclusive yet (for example, there are some free platforms, but they're limited) but that will likely change as the technology continues to advance.

Some general uses of AI include having students evaluate AI-generated content in small group discussions, or use AI to help them organize their own ideas. AI can be used for brainstorming and for proofreading. AI can also be used to create practice exercises, quizzes, or study guides, which give students the opportunity to reinforce their own learning. Consider a major like computer science, for example. Xin Ye (Assistant Professor, Rockland Community College) plans to integrate AI into her courses in the fall 2023 semester. Students can use AI to receive feedback or corrections while they are coding.

In-Class Activities

Here are four sample in-class activities created by Racheal Fest (SUNY Oneonta; The Faculty Center for Teaching, Learning, and Scholarship Specialist in Pedagogy) that would introduce students to AI literacy in a variety of disciplines:

Example 1: Prompt Engineering

This activity invites students to experiment and evaluate a range of prompting strategies with a particular output in mind. Students begin by prompting ChatGPT or Bing to generate a scholarly or popular essay on an assigned topic, likely one derived from shared course content (say, an example of panopticism inspired by Michel Foucault's well-known chapter).

Students should ask the AI tool to modify, correct, revise, or take a different approach to its output (for instance, *give me a different example*, or *simplify your explanation*, or *break this down into steps*. Online resources, including Wikipedia, list prompt intervention strategies). After students elicit several rounds of changes from the AI tool, they print a record of their engagement.

Finally, students can reflect on their process by assessing the efficacy of their own prompts and the quality of AI outputs. Did they manage to produce desired results? How? What strategies did they employ? How did they struggle? What does AI do well? What does AI do poorly?

Students could begin this work collectively, guided by an instructor who might elicit prompts and enter them into ChatGPT, Bing, etc., on a projector. After modeling this process and discussing prompting strategies, students could go on to complete individual assignments.

Example 2: Evaluating Form and Content of AI Outputs

This activity invites students to think critically about the strengths and challenges of content generated by both AI and other humans. First, students respond to a writing prompt relevant to course content without engaging generative AI.

Once they have completed the exercise, students enter the same writing prompt into ChatGPT, Bing, or another generative AI tool. Students then evaluate the texts, comparing and contrasting their formal features, their approaches to content, and more. What are the strengths and areas of growth for each? What differences and similarities do students notice? How does AI write? How do humans write? How could each improve their compositions and outputs?

Utah Tech University's Center for Teaching and Learning provides additional examples of rethinking learning outcomes with AI. Their [drop-down on Integrating AI in Teaching](#) offers several good suggestions. For example, instead of asking nursing students to summarize research on evidence-based practice, they might compare an AI-generated summary and a summary written by a human to see what the differences are (and therefore, how that could change the outcomes of that scenario).

Example 3: Using AI for Brainstorming and Idea Development

AI can be used as a brainstorming tool to help undergraduates narrow down their ideas for research or to come up with initial ideas.. In a recent Alchemy webinar, "Harnessing the Power of AI: Transforming Assignments and Assessments in Higher Education", Dr. Danny Liu (University of Sydney) suggested using ChatGPT this way: have the students encourage the chatbot to ask them questions and generate text based on their responses. The following example comes from a direct exchange with ChatGPT from Stephanie Pritchard's (SUNY Oswego) English composition class:

Prompt: I have to write a research paper about a community I belong to and how it uses literacy for my English composition college class. Can you ask me some questions to help me brainstorm for the assignment?

AI: Certainly! Brainstorming is a crucial step in the research process. Here are some questions to help you explore how your community uses literacy and generate ideas for your research paper:

1. What is the specific community you belong to, and how would you define it?
2. How does your community value literacy, and what role does it play in daily life?
3. What are the various forms of literacy within your community? (e.g., reading, writing, digital literacy, cultural literacy)
4. Are there particular literacy practices or traditions unique to your community?
5. How does literacy impact communication within your community? Does it influence how members interact and express themselves?

6. Are there any challenges or barriers related to literacy in your community? (e.g., access to education, language differences, technological limitations)

The AI created 13 additional questions that we did not include here. Students can request that the AI ask one question at a time so they can respond to each one or provide a list so they can consider their options. And with more practice with prompt engineering, students can refine their questions and get even better at asking the AI for help.

Example 4: Using AI for Proofreading

Proofreading often gets neglected by students because it is time-consuming, boring, or they feel that there is not enough time to do it before an assignment is due. In addition to built-in spell checkers in programs like Microsoft and Google, many students also use Grammarly to help them with sentence structure, tone, etc. Students can use ChatGPT for proofreading as well.

For example, pasting a text into the chatbot and simply asking "Can you proofread this for me?" will yield different results than pasting in text with more specific requests like, "Can you identify the analysis in this history paper?" or "Please describe the counterclaim in this argumentative essay." Students can then compare what the generative AI tool noted and see if they are achieving what they mean to in their writing.

AI can help students in other ways as well: for example, if students are writing in the sciences, they may be required to use passive voice. Asking ChatGPT to specifically check a text for active voice would be a helpful activity. Students can also ask ChatGPT to check their citations or to evaluate their introductory or conclusion paragraphs. However, they should be advised and reminded that generative AI can and does make errors and suggest erroneous information. Students must use their judgment before accepting generative AI suggestions.

Many of the major citation styles have adopted policies around citation and generative chatbots:

Citing generative AI in MLA Style

Citing generative AI in APA Style

Citing generative AI in Chicago Style

Writing Assignments

Here are two sample writing assignments created by Stephanie Pritchard (SUNY Oswego) that can be incorporated into a variety of disciplines:

Example 1: Reflective Process Book

While it will be very challenging now (read: almost impossible) to create out of class assignments that are "AI-proof", some assignments might be easier for students to complete without assistance from AI. One example would be a semester-long reflective process book, which is an assignment that can be used alongside research. The sample process book assignment that's linked here has a few notable features: it is graded mostly based on completion (this assessment strategy might lesson some of the grade anxiety faced by many undergraduate students), it is meant to be completed in stages (students will also have some time to work on this in class), and it is meant to be reflective (so students can describe what they learned but, more importantly, how they learned it). The process book asks students to think critically about their own research, discussions in class, and the steps they took to complete their research assignment. This assignment can be a strong addition to classes that require critical thinking, writing, and discussion. The process book assignment linked here is from an English composition class.

Example 2: Annotated Bibliography

There are also ways to integrate AI into research-based assignments, like an annotated bibliography. This annotated bibliography example, from an English composition class, asks students to find and evaluate six different credible sources for their research project. For every source, students must provide bibliographic information, a short summary, an evaluation of the source, and a brief discussion of how the source is relevant to their topic. There is a note at the bottom of this assignment which outlines what parts of the annotated bibliography can receive help from AI: to create appropriate citations, to help look for sources, and to help students understand the content of the sources they're considering. Since annotated bibliographies are popular assignments, there are various ways generative AI tools can be used to simplify the process for students as they begin to learn how to conduct research, especially in introductory classes.

What we've learned from AI so far is that it can write reflectively – and convincingly – about experiences that it can absorb from the data on which it was trained but cannot actually have first-hand. The process book is meant to help students critically think about how they learned. It's worth mentioning, too, that both of these assignments are part of a larger, semester-long scaffolded writing project.

Some additional out-of-class examples include rethinking reading response papers and other essay assignments.

AI Tools for Research Assignments

As generative AI tools proliferate, more special-purpose tools are being released for use. One such tool for annotated bibliographies and research-related assignments is elicit.org. Asking a question such as "What is the current interpretation of the cause of mid-latitude glaciers on Mars?" returns a list of relevant papers with bibliographic information and short summaries, along with a summary of the top papers which provides a snapshot of the field of research. Clicking on the title of any of the papers opens a new window with the full text of the paper, summary information, factors reflecting the trustworthiness of the paper, critiques listed in other sources, and related citations. The research landscape is likely to change rapidly with the further development of specialized generative AI tools.

Lab Reports

A typical college-level lab report structure includes an abstract, introduction, procedure, analysis, results, discussion, and conclusion. Some high school students may have experience with lab reports, but college-level writing is often more complex.

Dr. Trevor Johnson-Steigelman (Associate Professor, Finger Lakes Community College) suggests an activity you can introduce early in the semester by providing your students with a model lab report (this example can also be used to demonstrate your expectations and serve as a guide for your students).

Students can use generative AI to write abstracts or conclusions for lab reports by inputting their lab report's main body into the generator. As we mentioned earlier, it can be a helpful activity for students to compare their own abstracts or conclusions to what the AI produces. AI can summarize key findings, and AI-generated results may offer valuable insights by helping students see what they may have missed.

As with many of the assignments and activities suggested here, it is important to encourage your students to continue to think for themselves instead of copying results into a final report: to focus on the process of evaluation and quality of sources, rather than the outcome alone.

Accessibility

The Accessibility Resources offices on many college campuses have seen a huge increase in numbers over the last couple of years. In addition to offering accommodations like extended time on exams, preferred classroom seating, and food allergy or dietary restrictions, many offices also have technology for students as well. Some examples of assistive technology include smart pens, recording devices, and speech-to-text software.

AI tools have begun to make big impacts on digital accessibility (the practice of designing and developing digital content that people with disabilities can use). This means that people with visual, hearing, cognitive, or motor impairments can have access to these tools, which promotes inclusivity and more equal opportunities. However, concerns about student use of AI tools to cheat and the policies that result could restrict the ability of disabled students to use AI tools to support their learning (McMurtrie, 2023).

Here are some examples of what AI tools can do (Alston, 2023):

- Create captions for videos
- Use speech to text or text to speech
- Test accessibility of various websites
- Offer language translation or transcription

Some of the tools are free (like Google's Speech-to-text API and also Microsoft's Azure Speech to Text) but many are still quite limited unless users choose to upgrade to a paid version.

Considerations for Online Classes

Teaching online, whether synchronously or asynchronously, involves many of the same issues concerning student use of generative AI as are found when teaching in-person classes. Syllabus statements are important to clarify acceptable uses of generative AI, and faculty should anticipate questions such as:

- What constitutes plagiarism?
- What is the policy on the use of AI tools like ChatGPT , Grammarly, GitHub Copilot, DALL-E, Google translate, etc.?
- How do you cite ChatGPT?

Rethinking the online course learning objectives and the related online assignments and assessments in the age of ChatGPT is now an essential aspect of preparing to teach online.

To best support online learners' success, assignments should be designed to make critical thinking and the process of learning visible to the online course instructor and online classmates. Scaffolded assignments with feedback are more effective than just asking for a paper, or essay, as a completed final product in one step. These considerations will be especially important for asynchronous online classes. Synchronous online classes have the option to include Lane 1 activities (as described above) to assure student attainment of course learning outcomes through real-time activities and interactions. Asynchronous online courses have no built-in option for such Lane 1 activities and must rely more heavily on scaffolded learning activities that focus on the learning process more than the learning product.

Here are some recommendations for effective online teaching practices:

- Design assignments that must reference weekly course readings, content, and online interactions/discussions.
- If applicable, incorporate or ask online learners to incorporate very recent news and current events into assignments (there will be a lag in between the time a news event occurs and when it is added to AI language models, although how long is likely to decrease as time goes on).
- Prompt learners to incorporate their own personal views, experiences, examples, or aspirations into their assignments.
- Design assignments that build toward a final product, one step at a time.
- Allow online learners options in how they make their thinking and learning visible to you. For example, design activities where learners can create a multimedia response to an assignment.

AI Tools Can Support Teaching: Examples

AI tools are useful for faculty as well as for students. One use of these tools is to generate ideas and content for our courses. Below are examples from Dr. Keith Landa (SUNY Purchase, Director of the Teaching, Learning, and Technology Center) and Stephanie Pritchard (SUNY Oswego).

Example 1: Course Design

Dr. Landa wanted to use Claude, an generative AI generator, to see what course learning objectives he might consider for a new class on AI Literacy. Here's his exchange:

Prompt: "As a higher education faculty member designing a course on AI Literacy, what would be the top learning outcomes that you would list in your syllabus?"

AI: Here are some potential key learning outcomes I would aim for in a course focused on AI literacy:

- Understand fundamental concepts of artificial intelligence – e.g. machine learning, neural networks, data dependence, training vs. inference.
- Recognize common applications of AI – such as computer vision, natural language processing, recommender systems, robotics.
- Evaluate societal impacts of AI – economic, legal, ethical issues surrounding use cases.
- Detect misinformation about AI capabilities – critically assess claims in media/marketing vs reality.
- Analyze AI risks and mitigation strategies – e.g. data bias, job automation, legal liability, superintelligence.
- Discuss governance challenges – privacy, accountability, transparency, oversight.
- Consider philosophical questions – machine consciousness, human-AI relationships, AI existential risk.
- Empower learners as citizens – understand basics to follow policy issues, separate hype from reality, advocate responsibly.
- Hands-on experience – interact with AI models, experiment with sample projects, complete risk assessment.

AI: The goal would be to not just impart technical knowledge but also develop students' critical thinking on the real-world impacts of AI. Focusing on risks and responsible innovation priorities would equip learners to participate ethically and intelligently in our AI-integrated world.

There are too many more learning outcomes here for a single course, so this list would need to be focused and refined to settle on the appropriate learning objectives for an AI Literacy course. But this is a good start, and faculty can ask the AI for more details to begin brainstorming class activities to these outcomes (i.e. – "What learning activities and assessments would you map onto the learning outcomes listed above?"). AI could also help faculty begin to assemble a list of course resources (i.e. – "What textbooks, articles, web videos, and other learning resources would you assign for this class?"). Of course, faculty will still need to carefully vet the AI's response to ensure the AI is providing reliable information. This article from _The New York Times_ [provides additional information about generative AI and its hallucinations](#).

Example 2: Developing Question Banks for Formative Testing

This LinkedIn post ["Yes, ChatGPT can answer exam questions. But can it write them too?"](#) provides an interesting example of how ChatGPT integrates different levels of Bloom's taxonomy to write multiple choice questions on natural selection. However, this sort of one-off question generation is not an efficient approach to generating a large test bank of questions for use in repeated formative testing.

Here's an example of the kind of prompt Dr. Landa has used to create test bank questions for a class he's offered previously:

> Please write 10 multiple choice questions based on the content at this web page, https://astrobiology.com/1998/04/what-is-astrobiology.htm, targeted at the remembering level of Bloom's taxonomy, and provide the correct answer for each.

Dr. Landa has used this prompt in the [free version of ChatGPT](#) and also in [Claude](#); both chatbots recognize and can correctly reference the different levels of Bloom's taxonomy and both are able to access the content using the external URL.

Dr. Landa also altered the prompt to generate questions at the "analyzing" level of Bloom's taxonomy. While it is still necessary to review the questions that are produced by the chatbots, this approach makes it much easier for us to set up learning activities to promote ongoing retrieval practice by our students.

To use AI for generating sample questions for PDF articles that are used in class, faculty can use tools that allow file uploads (like Claude) or that allow them to copy and paste in large source texts.

Example 3: Creating Rubrics

Some course-related material, like rubrics, can be extremely time-consuming to create, and generative AI can help faculty speed up that process. While AI won't be able to create a perfect rubric on the first try, users can modify prompts to get a better template.

Here's an example based on an assignment that Stephanie Pritchard (SUNY Oswego) created to assess student writing at the end of a summer Educational Opportunity Program (EOP). The assignment has been condensed to save space:

Prompt: Create a rubric to assess the following writing assignment: The purpose of writing persuasively is to get your reader to agree with your opinion. You have more freedom to make claims without always using research to back up what you're saying.

What grade do you think you should receive for the summer program? You can use any examples from the program to make your point, but you should choose at least two reasons from your EOP experience to answer this question. Here are some options for you to consider (you are not limited to this list):

- your class attendance and class participation (including reading workshops, writing workshops, etc.)
- grades you received on major assignments
- your attendance and participation at social events as well as your general attitude during the program
- what you've learned (or not learned) from this experience

How you approach this is totally up to you – your tone can be formal or informal, funny or serious, creative or more traditional. Effective persuasive writing always has a purpose in mind.

AI: Criteria | Excellent (5) | Good (4) | Satisfactory (3) | Needs Improvement (2) | Inadequate (1)

Claim | The writer clearly | The writer's | The writer's claim | The writer's claim | The writer's claim | states their | claim states | is somewhat clear | lacks clarity or | lacks clarity and | position on the | their position| but may require | specificity, making it | specificity, and | grade they should | on the grade | further elaboration | challenging to | does not take a | receive and is | they should | or additional | understand their | clear stance on | persuasive with | receive, but | examples to | intended grade or | the grade they | compelling | might benefit | strengthen the | should receive. | arguments. | from more | reasons for it. |
| | elaboration. | | | | | | strengthen the | argument. |

The AI's first attempt at the rubric was hard to follow (it generated six additional paragraphs that looked like different versions of this on the following topics: use of examples, organization, persuasiveness, tone and style, and overall impact). Professor Pritchard decided to refine the prompt a little more:

Prompt: I find the formatting of your response confusing. Can you answer the same prompt but format your response differently?

AI: Sure! Let's break down the rubric in a more straightforward and easy-to-read format:

Claim:

- Excellent (5): The writer's claim is clear, persuasive, and well-defined, taking a strong stance on the grade they should receive. Compelling arguments are presented.
- Good (4): The writer's claim is clear, but may benefit from further elaboration or more compelling arguments.
- Satisfactory (3): The writer's claim is somewhat clear, but lacks specificity and may require additional examples to strengthen the argument.
- Needs Improvement (2): The writer's claim lacks clarity and specificity, making it challenging to understand their intended grade or reasons for it.
- Inadequate (1): The writer fails to take a clear stance on the grade they should receive.

Use of Examples:

- Excellent (5): The writer effectively uses specific examples from the EOP program to support their claim, making their persuasive writing more convincing.
- Good (4): The writer incorporates relevant examples from the EOP program to support their claim, but might benefit from stronger connections between examples and arguments.
- Satisfactory (3): The writer includes some relevant examples from the EOP program, but their connection to the claim may be somewhat unclear or disjointed.
- Needs Improvement (2): The writer provides limited or irrelevant examples to support their claim, weakening the persuasiveness of their writing.
- Inadequate (1): The writer does not include any examples to support their claim, significantly weakening their persuasive writing.

While these two examples aren't perfect, the chatbot was able to establish some general parameters and provided ideas about what parts of the assignment could be assessed. The AI initially suggested assessing based on the following criteria: claim, use of examples, organization, persuasiveness, tone and style, and overall impact. Professor Pritchard decided to ask the chatbot for some additional suggestions:

Prompt: I like the claim, use of examples, and organization points, but found persuasiveness and tone/style to not be as necessary. Can you come up with a few other points that we might consider when assessing student writing for this assignment?

AI: Certainly! Here are a few additional points that you might consider when assessing student writing for this assignment:

Engagement:

- Excellent (5): Keeps the reader engaged throughout the writing with a compelling introduction, thought-provoking points, and an effective conclusion.
- Good (4): Maintains reader's interest but might benefit from a more captivating introduction or stronger conclusion.
- Satisfactory (3): Some engagement, but the writing may lack a consistent flow and reader interest.
- Needs Improvement (2): Fails to engage the reader effectively due to disjointed points or weak conclusion.
- Inadequate (1): Lacks any form of engagement.

Clarity:

- Excellent (5): Ideas are expressed clearly and concisely, making the writing easy to follow.
- Good (4): Generally clear, but some points could use further clarification.
- Satisfactory (3): Ideas are somewhat clear, but the writing might be confusing or overly verbose in places.
- Needs Improvement (2): Lack of clarity, reader struggles to understand key points due to poor expression.
- Inadequate (1): Extremely unclear, ideas are virtually impossible to comprehend.

Creativity:

- Excellent (5): Demonstrates a high level of creativity in approach, examples, and presentation.
- Good (4): Shows creativity, but could benefit from more original ideas or approaches.
- Satisfactory (3): Some attempt at creativity, but the writing may feel somewhat predictable.
- Needs Improvement (2): Lacks creativity and originality, ideas are mundane and unremarkable.
- Inadequate (1): Completely devoid of creativity.

PART IV
AI IN STUDENT RESEARCH AND CREATIVE WORKS

The Role of AI in the Student's Research/Creation Process

University faculty and the academic framework of the college environment play a critical role in facilitating the intellectual growth of the student researcher and demonstrating the cumulative scope of the research process, of which the students will ultimately become the drivers. Thus, faculty in supervisory research roles will need to be cognizant of how the use of artificial intelligence and generative models can both help and hinder the research process and growth of the researcher.

Although coursework can be more and less open-ended, there is typically a more defined and *a priori*-known result or conclusion inherent in the learning objectives required for a given course. Indeed, it may be that open-ended learning is a learning objective in some courses. Nonetheless, there is a distinct difference between coursework learning and the learning of the research process, namely that inherent in fundamental research is that the result is not known *a priori*; otherwise the result would not be a discovery. Thus, there are considerations unique to the research process that are important to highlight.

In this section, we discuss AI and generative models in the context of the intellectual growth of the student researcher, the development of research and scholarship, and the assessment of research and scholarship.

AI as it Pertains to the Intellectual Growth of the Student Researcher

There is a legacy of science and technology working in tandem in driving innovation and discovery. Scholars, researchers, engineers, and artists have been critical to this growth as they harness new technology. There are many implications of AI and generative models in this construct; we only point out several of them with respect to the research process here as the impacts and implications will evolve with the technology. As it pertains to the intellectual growth of the student researcher, whether undergraduate or graduate, two aspects that are highlighted are the insecurity or vulnerability that are inherent in the apprenticeship process of becoming an independent researcher and the leadership growth inherent in becoming an independent researcher.

While the research products of an undergraduate research project or thesis, a master's thesis, or a PhD dissertation are readily tangible, there is also, importantly, the intangible growth and scientific maturity that student researchers undergo as a part of earning their Masters or PhD. An example of this intellectual growth is the change from the initial insecurity of the student in their own knowledge that develops into confidence as the student researcher works through the process of the scientific method, deepens their foundational knowledge, and follows the data toward scientific understanding and becoming an independent contributor to the field. It is through the reliance on the fundamentals, the mathematics, the physics, and the observational constraints that the natural world is better understood, and the student matures to easily deciphering the boundaries of their knowledge and the knowledge that is yet to be discovered. As a part of the research process, the student researcher often becomes more self-aware, and in particular of their research strengths and weaknesses, often leveraging their strengths toward their unique contribution to the scientific domain.

In research pedagogy going forward, it will be important to ensure student researchers still have time to learn their own strengths and weaknesses. This is part of their intellectual growth wherein a researcher learns to leverage their strengths to realize their unique advancement of the field. It will be important that the student researcher does not rely too heavily on the use of AI and generative models in the early stages of their intellectual growth before their independent contribution to the discipline is recognized. . This may sound trivial, but it is a fundamental part of the research process. The scientific maturity gained as a part of this process also leads to leadership growth within a given scientific subdomain, thus springboarding the student to an advisory role for future projects in their career.

That said, the challenges inherent in personal and professional growth can be stymieing and overwhelming during the research process. There are many aspects of the process where AI and generative models can complement both student strengths and weaknesses as well as facilitate student growth and development. The idea generation component can aid students who overfocus on implementation, and the implementation aspects can help in streamlining and automating tasks for students who may have challenges moving from the idea/innovation stage to implementation.

Using AI to Develop Research and Scholarship

AI Literacy

Given the nature of AI, ironic as it may sound at first, teaching AI should, first and foremost, be about teaching students to retain their agency, and participate in the training of the tool/s themselves (Dai et al., 2023). With a platform like ChatGPT that is trained on the internet up to January 2022, if students aren't offered basic if not somewhat intermediate AI literacy training, by default, usage will rely too heavily on these nascent tools, and output will be suboptimal.

The teaching of AI literacy as it regards prompt engineering (or incremental prompting, breaking down larger goals into smaller tasks) though far from the norm, will be key moving forward (Lingard, 2023; Wallter, 2024). This includes submitting the writing i.e. the research under consideration and/or one's own research (from where the bulk of training is imparted), the purpose, audience, tone, and length. These criteria will help researchers connect the dots between their agency (training, prompting, critical thinking) and the end results.

Opportunities

Opportunities for the use of AI can be found in all stages of the research process, beginning with idea generation, working through literature reviews, identifying and preparing data, determining and implementing testing frameworks and analyzing results (Xames and Shefa, 2023). Tasks involved in getting funding for research, including writing funding proposals, are also prime candidates. AI may not only assist with these tasks, it is also being considered as a primary actor in them (Messeri and Crockett, 2024; Bano et. al., 2023).

AI has certainly already been tagged for its ability to offer research assistance, be it for faculty or students.. Circling back to the topic of agency in the AI interface, several new AI tools are basing output on required input (ie. pdf's), giving researchers the ability to train the tool as they use it (e.g. Humata, ChatPDF, Research Rabbit). There are other AI tools whose generative capacity is already trained on specific scholarly writing [read: not the entire internet up to 2022] (e.g. Elicit, Scite, Consensus). And as with most AI tool platforms, providing a login typically enables usage history to be logged, and in the more adept tools, collections to be created, a user profile etched, with tailored and trained output to follow, not wholly different from a commercial web browser.

Risks

All of the risks that come along with AI tools in other domains follow them to the research domain. Most of these risks apply to traditional forms of research as well, but have new sources and take new forms when AI is involved. Bias may be introduced through missing and incomplete data sets as well as through the algorithms that are used to train the AI models (Bano et al, 2023). (Several types of bias are explained in Appendix B.) There are ethical concerns regarding the source of the data used to train the models and whether it has been appropriately credited, as well as questions about how to ensure the fairness and reproducibility of research was conducted with the use of (or entirely by) AI. As AI is relied upon more and more, there are risks of reproducing old patterns of excluding diverse perspectives and biases, while making it increasingly difficult to identify and distinguish when this is happening (Messeri & Crockett, 2024; Shah, C. 2024). With all of this in mind, the European Commission has released a downloadable set of [Living guidelines on the responsible use of generative AI in research](#) based on reliability, honesty, respect, and accountability (Directorate-General for Research and Innovation, 2024).

And although the question of how to develop a student's confidence and independence in their scientific maturity is not new, the easy access to tools which appear to be able to do the act of research for them introduces significant new implications. Students may not be confident about their contributions. It will be important to consider that:

- As part of the research process, students are learning and using the foundational principles to guide new discoveries; how will AI affect this?.
- We need to make sure students are still seeing their value and having their own original thoughts and contributions.
- We need to find the balance between using the tools and developing students' own skills and strengths.
- Student agency is retained.

One new risk is in the area of privacy. Traditional research methods and processes closely guard the importance of intellectual property for ideas before they are published. Normally a thesis might be embargoed, for example. New structures will need to be developed and put in place to address questions of how to apply similar constraints in a world in which ideas might be ingested into AI models during the research process, whether inadvertently or intentionally, before they are ready to be shared.

Citing/Disclosing

As with any other source, it is essential that AI is cited and disclosed clearly. Several common citation resources now include guidance on citing information derived from generative AI. Some recent examples follow, although these standards are still evolving and should not be considered normative:

APA Style Example Text and Reference

Text

When prompted with "Is the left brain right brain divide real or a metaphor?" the ChatGPT-generated text indicated that although the two brain hemispheres are somewhat specialized, "the notation that people can be characterized as 'left-brained' or 'right-brained' is considered to be an oversimplification and a popular myth" (OpenAI, 2023).

Reference

OpenAI. (2023). ChatGPT (Mar 14 version) [Large language model]. https://chat.openai.com/chat

MLA Style Example Text and Reference

Text

While the green light in The Great Gatsby might be said to chiefly symbolize four main things: optimism, the unattainability of the American dream, greed, and covetousness ("Describe the symbolism"), arguably the most important—the one that ties all four themes together—is greed.

Reference

"Describe the symbolism of the green light in the book The Great Gatsby by F. Scott Fitzgerald" prompt. ChatGPT, 13 Feb. version, OpenAI, 8 Mar. 2023, chat.openai.com/chat.

(Citation information is derived from the Harvard LibGuide on Citing Generative AI, which was itself adapted from a LibGuide created by Daniel Xiao, Research Impact Librarian at Texas A&M University Libraries.)

Using AI to Evaluate Research and Scholarship

Funder and Publisher Guidelines

In addition to the use of AI to create and publish research, there are countless opportunities for its use in the act of evaluating research and scholarship. It's important to be aware of the rules that apply to its use. In December, 2023, the National Science Foundation published guidelines prohibiting reviewers from uploading contents of research proposals (and related material) to "non-approved Generative AI tools" (*Notice to Research Community*, 2023). Journal publishers are also developing policies for peer-review. For example, the journal *Nature*, as of the time of this writing, requests that peer reviewers not upload manuscripts into generative AI tools and that they disclose the use of AI tools if they were used in any way in evaluation of the reviewed material (*Artificial Intelligence (AI) | Nature Portfolio, n.d.*). These policies will continue to evolve – check for the latest information before embarking on the use of AI in any activity involving the evaluation of research and scholarship.

Using AI in Creative Works

The implications of generative AI for creative fields span across visual arts, design, film, television, performing arts, writing, and media industries, with potential affordances and concerns in both the process of creation and the industries at large. As in other fields, generative AI can automate repetitive tasks and provide efficiencies, access, and a speeding up of processes that allow for new possibilities in art, design, performance, and across media. However, the very concept of AI-generated art challenges current creation models, raises questions around authorship, authenticity, and ownership of creative works, is leading to reimagining how we define originality, and may put employees in creative industries, including creators, at significant risk of job loss and replacement. Generative AI raises new copyright and attribution issues, with the creative industry, courts, and regulators still navigating how it will affect the future of copyright and attribution (Holloway, Cheng, and Dickenson, 2024) (Appel, Neelbauer, and Schweidel, 2023).

Creative AI tools are proliferating that will facilitate every imaginable aspect of creative and composition processes, whether this be in visual arts, design, writing, music composition, filmmaking, video, or other fields. These delve into the most minute aspect of complex creative and technical tasks in ways that were once only available through human collaborators – and in some ways, not previously possible. Tasks such as proof-reading, editing, creating drafts and proofs-of-concept, iterative refinement and the integration of new works, information and tools are made possible within minutes.

In the visual arts and design, generative AI is seen as a powerful tool that can automate repetitive tasks, such as resizing and cropping images, while ensuring design consistency and quality. It can accelerate conceptualization, prototyping, and design verification, making these processes faster and more cost-effective. This technology has also led to collaborations between AI and artists, blending human creativity with AI's capabilities to produce novel artworks that challenge traditional perceptions of art and creativity. For example, AI has been used to generate "Dali-like" images, which were then turned into three-dimensional objects through 3D printing and casting in bronze, highlighting the blend of AI capabilities and human craftsmanship (Shulman, 2024). AI can be applied to architectural design to address challenges and conceive innovative solutions. By inputting specific parameters such as materials, site conditions, and budget constraints, generative AI can quickly offer multiple design options that meet those requirements. This not only accelerates the design process but also opens up new avenues for creativity and collaboration. Despite its potential, challenges such as ensuring the feasibility and aesthetic quality of generated designs remain (Hakimshafaei, 2023, Houhou, 2023).

In film, television, and media production, generative AI promises to streamline video production through automated transcripts, video tagging, predictive editing, and real-time feedback, potentially enhancing efficiency in post-production and cross-platform optimization. In writing and literature, generative AI tools like language models have started assisting with content creation, offering new ways to brainstorm ideas, draft stories, and even generate entire narratives. Emerging applications of AI in music composition and the music industry are rapidly transforming how music is created, produced, and consumed. AI-powered tools are enhancing efficiency in audio processing tasks such as drum track alignment, vocal tuning, noise reduction, and audio quality enhancement during mixing and mastering stages. Online services like LANDR utilize AI algorithms for audio track analysis and adjustments, providing affordable and high-quality mastering services to artists without extensive audio engineering knowledge. The integration of AI in music production has also led to the development of virtual instruments and vocal synthesizers capable of producing realistic sounds (Steen and Lux, 2024). Generative AI applications in music composition are expanding into areas like media production, interactive music experiences, remixing, music production, and sound design. These applications are fostering new forms of creative expression and enabling composers to explore novel musical ideas with the support of AI (STL Digital, 2024).

Copyright, Intellectual Property and Applications in Creative Industries

Recent union negotiations involving authors, actors, and film workers have placed a significant emphasis on the use of artificial intelligence (AI) in their industries. These discussions have centered around concerns related to job security, copyright, and the ethical use of AI in creative work. The Writers Guild of America (WGA) successfully concluded negotiations with Hollywood Studios, addressing the use of AI in the writing process. The agreement ensures that AI cannot be used to write or rewrite scripts and that AI-generated writing will not be considered source material. Moreover, individual writers retain the choice to use AI tools, but companies cannot mandate their use (WGA 2023). SAG-AFTRA, the union representing film and TV performers, announced a deal with Replica Studios concerning the use of AI in voice acting, specifically in video games. This agreement establishes protections for digitally replicated voices, requiring consent from performers before their voices can be used and allowing them to opt out of continuous use in future projects (SAG-AFTRA 2024). The Author's Guild has been very aggressive about pursuing the rights of authors in relation to the use of generative AI to train, reproduce or imitate authored works (The Authors Guild Bulletin, 2023). The Guild provides a guidance page on AI Best Practices for authors. They include the following suggestions for using generative AI ethically:

1. Use AI as an assistant for brainstorming, editing, and refining ideas rather than a primary source of work, with the goal of maintaining the unique spirit that defines human creativity. Use AI to support, not replace, this process.
2. To the extent you use AI to generate text, be sure to rewrite it in your own voice before adopting it. If you are claiming authorship, then you should be the author of your work.
3. If an appreciable amount of AI-generated text, characters, or plot are incorporated in your manuscript, you must disclose it to your publisher and should also disclose it to the reader. We don't think it is necessary for authors to disclose generative AI use when it is employed merely as a tool for brainstorming, idea generation, or for copyediting.
4. Respect the rights of other writers when using generative AI technologies, including copyrights, trademarks, and other rights, and do not use generative AI to copy or mimic the unique styles, voices, or other distinctive attributes of other writers' works in ways that harm the works. (Note: doing so could also be subject to claims of unfair competition).
5. Thoroughly review and fact-check all content generated by AI systems. As of now, you cannot trust the accuracy of any factual information provided by generative AI. All Chatbots now available make information up. They are text-completion tools, not information tools. Also, be aware and check for potential biases in the AI output, be they gender, racial, socioeconomic, or other biases that could perpetuate harmful stereotypes or misinformation.
6. Show solidarity with and support professional creators in other fields, including voice actors and narrators, translators, illustrators, etc., as they also need to protect their professions from generative AI uses. (The Authors Guild, 2024)

Generative AI in Student Creative Works

Generative AI tools can serve to foster creativity, innovation, and efficiency in students' projects; yet they also necessitate a mindful approach to their integration into educational practices. In design and arts, for example, AI-generated prototypes can serve as starting points for discussions about aesthetic, functional, and technical considerations. Similarly, in writing and music, AI-generated samples can illustrate how different styles or elements might alter the perception of a piece, thereby deepening students' understanding of their craft. By integrating generative AI into student work, students will be prepared for a future in which these tools will likely play a significant role in creative industries. Familiarity with AI tools and an understanding of their potential and limitations will equip students with the skills necessary to navigate the future job market and contribute to the evolution of their fields. While generative AI can automate certain aspects of the creative process, we should emphasize the irreplaceable value of human creativity, judgment, and ethical considerations.

Encouraging students to use AI as a tool to augment their work rather than replace the creative process can help maintain this balance. This approach ensures that AI serves to enhance student learning and creativity while acquiring essential skills, including AI fluency in their field. Faculty will need to establish clear guidelines on the ethical use of generative AI in student creative work. This includes understanding copyright and attribution, emphasizing the importance of originality, and encouraging students to critically engage with AI-generated content as part of their creative process, not as the endpoint. Discussions around the potential biases inherent in AI models and the importance of critical, human oversight in the creative process are also crucial.

Summary and Additional Considerations

The use of AI and generative models has the ability to greatly propel research and discovery. How and where the models are used in the research process will likely be both systematic and individualized across and within disciplines. Thus, there are expected to be commonalities and great variabilities in how research has been traditionally done and how AI is going to change the process. Identifying where it can be particularly useful and where it might be less useful will likely be a research domain in and of itself, as well as how it impacts the student research growth process.

With the now massive amounts of data and information available, the need for sophisticated tools to help parse and analyze the information is paramount. Nonetheless, insights from humans will remain an integral part of the scientific research process. As described in a recent publication on AI and understanding in scientific research:

> "Training the next generation of scientists to identify and avoid the epistemic risks of AI will require not only technical education, but also exposure to scholarship in science and technology studies, social epistemology and philosophy of science" (Messeri & Crockett, 2024).

Additional topics that are expected to be relevant for future consideration of AI in the research process are leveraging AI to facilitate automated tasks in the research workflow (including administrative tasks like using AI to administer sponsored research), time management and in particular automated tasks, as well as complementing strengths and weaknesses for researchers in the research workflow. Each of these will require assessment of pros and cons for a given field or across disciplines, including preserving intellectual property for research still in its infancy or unpublished state.

PART V
EVALUATING AI TOOLS IN HIGHER EDUCATION

Student Evaluation Practices and Assessment Strategies

AI is going to drastically change how faculty perceive assessment and grading (Young, 2023), requiring them to rethink learning outcomes, redesign assignments (Stanford, 2023), and also consider more progressive approaches to student learning instead of more traditional methods.

This statement from CJ Yeh (Fashion Institute of Technology Professor of Communication Design Foundation) and Christie Shin (Fashion Institute of Technology Associate Professor of Communication Design Foundation) describes some of the changes that will need to be made within the field of design education:

> We will need a greater focus on interdisciplinary collaboration. In order to solve the increasingly complex problems that contemporary society is facing today, it is critical for aspiring designers to learn how to collaborate effectively with developers, engineers, and other stakeholders. This means students will need to communicate effectively, share ideas, and work together to achieve common goals. Some key learning objectives would include the following:

1. Critical thinking and problem framing: AI can accomplish many tasks, but it cannot replace creativity, critical thinking, and (most importantly!) empathy. Students need to learn how to use these skills to accurately define problems and come up with new solutions.
2. Cloud-based remote collaboration: These tools are essential for designers who want to work efficiently and effectively with team members who are located in different places and other fields. Designers can share files, communicate in real time, and track progress on projects from the comfort of their own homes or offices.
3. AI-assisted design process: Students need to learn how to use AI technologies, including using AI to automate tasks, generate ideas, and test designs.
4. Ethics and social responsibility: We must stop focusing on simply teaching students how to create the most persuasive ads, seductive designs, addictive games, etc. The next generation of designers needs to learn about the ethical implications of design and social responsibility. This includes learning about privacy, accessibility, and sustainability.

AI's Impact on Summative Assessment: An Example

In an Alchemy webinar titled "Harnessing the Power of AI: Transforming Assignments and Assessments in Higher Education, Dr. Danny Liu (University of Sydney) discussed the importance of designing authentic assessments (Villarroel et al., 2017) and the importance of feedback (Carless & Boud, 2018).

The Villarroel et al. study suggests that faculty make assessment more like real-world tasks students might encounter in a future job. Students tend to learn better, feel more motivated, and feel like they are managing their own learning. The study suggests a step-by-step model to help faculty create their own authentic assessments in higher education.

Carless and Boud discuss student feedback literacy, which is how students are able to understand and use feedback to improve their work and learning. The paper focuses on how students respond to feedback and some challenges they face when applying feedback. Carless & Boud offer two activities that can help students improve their feedback literacy: giving feedback to each other and analyzing examples of good work.

Dr. Liu suggests a Two-Lane Approach in regard to assessment strategies with all of this in mind: how it's important to have some kind of "Lane 1" (read: traditional assessment to ensure learning outcomes are being met) approach, but how "Lane 2" would factor in the authentic assessment that students would be more motivated to complete. He uses this example in his presentation to demonstrate the approach:

Short and Longer Term Assessment Strategies

Lane 1: Assurance of Learning Outcomes	Lane 2: Human-AI Collaboration
Short term: - In-person exams/tests - Viva voces [oral exams]	Short term: - Students use AI to brainstorm, draft outlines, summarize resources, perform research - Students critique AI responses
Longer term: - In-class contemporaneous assessment - Interactive oral assessments - In-person exams/tests (sparingly)	Longer term: - Students collaborate with AI and document this process; the process is graded more heavily than the product

The idea is to try to find balance between traditional assessment methods and new ways to assess student learning by encouraging their collaboration with AI. Dr. Liu provided an example from a marketing class.

Example of a Two-Lane Approach

Learning outcomes: apply marketing strategy concepts in real-world scenarios; demonstrate communication skills; evaluate effectiveness of different strategies.

Further Assessment Strategies

Lane 1: Assurance of Learning Outcomes	Lane 2: Human-AI Collaboration
Live Q&A after in-class presentation (defend research/analysis, etc.) Giving students unseen case study in a live unsupervised setting	Bing Chat for market research and competitor analysis Adobe Firefly for campaign design Collaboration process is documented (fact-checking, improving, critiquing) In-class presentation Process heavily weighted

In this example, the Lane 2 approach has more components as well as several opportunities for interaction with AI technology. Bing Chat is an AI-powered search engine, Adobe Firefly is an AI that can generate images, and students would have the opportunity to use other AI tools that could help generate text.

Process plays a big role in Dr. Liu's scenario (see the process book assignment in the next section), and there's more at stake for students in the Lane 1 assessment.

Alternative Grading Strategies

Alternative grading strategies that have become more popular over the last several years may help faculty think about evaluation in new ways and can reduce students' perceived need to use generative AI tools inappropriately. These include specifications grading, contract or labor-based grading, and ungrading. Each method is summarized below, along with links to additional information.

Specifications grading

Instructors create assignments with clearly specified requirements and assignments either meet the criteria or they don't. Revision opportunities are built in.

Contract grading/labor-based grading

Students and instructors agree to a contract in which each grade is tied to a set of criteria like allowed absences, the number of drafts or assignments completed in a satisfactory manner, and the number of reading responses submitted over the semester.

Ungrading

The instructor specifies learning objectives, and self-reflection is used regularly for students to self-assess their progress (in reflective journals, blogs, etc.). Instructors provide students with regular feedback, and midterm or final grades are determined by consultation between the instructor and the students.

Challenges with AI Detection Products

When AI turned into a buzzword early in 2023, there was a lot of discussion about different AI detectors and their effectiveness, including one called GPTZero. Some of these tools claim to be up to 99% accurate, but AI has also suggested that human-generated text is the result of chatbots when it is not. In June, Turnitin publicly acknowledged that its software has a higher false positive rate than the company originally stated. In July, OpenAI pulled its detection tool, AI Classifier, because of its "low rate of accuracy" (Nelson 2023). False positive results can have negative impacts for students, as seen in the example of a Texas A&M professor who suspected his students were using AI to cheat on their final essays. He copied essays into ChatGPT to determine whether or not his students were cheating and gave out incomplete grades to students in his class, which caused serious problems for graduating seniors, including many who had in fact not used AI on their assignments.

In addition to the false positives, many AI detectors are biased against non-native writers, as discussed in this paper by Liang et al. (2023). The book AI for Diversity, by Roger Søraa discusses a wide range of bias in varied ways, including gender, age, sexuality, etc.

There are also some opinions that it will be easy to "catch" students who use AI tools because AI technology doesn't sound human. While that may have been the case early on, these language models improve each time someone plugs in a new prompt. This article in the Chronicle got a lot of attention a few months ago when a student described how many of their peers were using this technology and challenging the notion about academic integrity policies. Consider how the story begins: "Submit work that reflects your own thinking or face discipline. A year ago, this was just about the most common-sense rule of Earth. Today, it's laughably naive" (Terry, 2023). Faculty need to assume that at least some students are going to seek out this technology.

Some faculty members may choose a more hands-on approach to AI-generated work. For example, if they suspect a student has used AI to produce work for an assignment, they might invite that student to have a one-on-one conversation and ask the student to explain their paper. In any case, it is especially important for faculty not to accuse students outright, as that will result in a lack of trust and will cause students to lose confidence and motivation to complete the course.

So what does this mean for AI detection software at this point? It means faculty can't rely on detectors. Given all of this, it is even more important to design assignments with AI in mind – by integrating these tools into assignments, faculty can teach students how to use them ethically.

Strategies for Pedagogical Evaluation

Once a potential tool has been identified for use in courses or programs, faculty should evaluate the tool prior to implementation. Evaluating an artificial intelligence tool for use in a higher education course requires a systematic approach to ensure its effectiveness and suitability for the educational context. Here's a step-by-step guide for evaluating such a tool:

1. **Define Learning Objectives:** Determine how the AI tool can complement or enhance the achievement of course learning objectives.
2. **Trial and Pilot Testing:** Conduct a trial or pilot test of the AI tool with a small group of students or colleagues. Gather feedback on its effectiveness and usability.
3. **Learning Analytics:** Assess the tool's ability to provide valuable learning analytics and insights for instructors and students. Analytics can help identify areas for improvement and measure learning outcomes.
4. **Feedback and Assessment:** Collect feedback from students who used the AI tool and assess its impact on their learning experience and outcomes.
5. **Integration with Curriculum:** Ensure the AI tool can be integrated seamlessly into the course curriculum without disrupting the overall flow of the course.
6. **Comparison with Traditional Methods:** Compare the AI tool's effectiveness with traditional teaching methods to gauge its added value.
7. **Support for Multimodal Learning:** Verify if the AI tool supports multimodal learning, allowing students to engage with content using various formats, such as text, audio, video, and interactive elements.
8. **Long-Term Viability:** Assess the long-term viability of the AI tool, considering its potential for future updates and scalability.

Strategies for Technology Evaluation

1. **Research and Identify AI Tools:** Conduct thorough research to identify various AI tools that align with course goals. Look for tools with good reviews, user feedback, and proven track records in education.
2. **Assess Features and Functionality:** Review the features and functionalities of each AI tool. Ensure that they align with your specific learning objective(s) and enhance the learning experience.
3. **User Interface and Experience:** Test the user interface of the AI tool to ensure it is intuitive and user-friendly. A complicated interface can hinder student engagement and learning.
4. **Data Privacy and Security:** Evaluate the AI tool's data privacy and security measures. Ensure that student data is protected and that the tool complies with relevant privacy regulations. 1EdTech's TrustEd Apps™ Generative AI Data Rubric (Data Privacy section) is a self-assessment tool for suppliers that is still in the early stages of development but may be useful in helping to identify the questions that need to be asked.
    a. **Data Collection and Storage:** Determine what data the AI tool collects from students and how it is stored. Ensure that personally identifiable information (PII) and sensitive data are handled securely and that data retention policies comply with relevant regulations.
        i. Determine if the data collected is used to train the tool and the potential impacts this may have on your teaching practice or students.
    b. **Vendor Policies and Agreements:** Carefully review the privacy policy and terms of service of the AI tool provider to understand how they handle student data and what responsibilities they hold.
    c. **Data Sharing:** Check if the AI tool shares student data with third parties or if it aggregates data across institutions. Be cautious about tools that may share data without explicit consent or for purposes beyond the scope of the educational context.
    d. **Data Anonymization and De-identification:** Verify if the AI tool anonymizes or de-identifies student data to protect their privacy. This is essential to prevent data breaches and unauthorized access.
    e. **Access Controls:** Check the access controls and permissions for the AI tool. Instructors should only have access to the data necessary for teaching, while students should have appropriate control over their personal information.
    f. **GDPR and Compliance:** If the AI tool operates in or collects data from users in the European Union, ensure that it complies with the General Data Protection Regulation (GDPR) and other relevant data protection laws.
    g. **Security Audits and Certifications:** Inquire whether the AI tool provider undergoes regular security audits and holds relevant certifications to ensure that their data protection practices meet industry standards.
    h. **Incident Response and Data Breach Policies:** Understand the AI tool provider's incident response plan and data breach policies. Be confident that they have processes in place to handle any potential security breaches promptly and responsibly.
    i. **Data Ownership and Portability:** Clarify who owns the data generated through the AI tool and ensure that students have the right to access and export their data if needed.
5. **Compatibility and Integration:** Check if the AI tool can integrate seamlessly with the existing learning management system or that it can be easily accessed.
6. **Vendor Reputation and Support:** Research the reputation of the AI tool's vendor. Consider factors like customer support, ongoing updates, and responsiveness to issues or concerns.
7. **Instructor Training and Support:** Consider the training and support provided to instructors in using the AI tool effectively.
8. **Institutional Approval and Policy Compliance:** Ensure that the AI tool meets institutional policies and guidelines for educational technology adoption. (The New York State Information Technology policy on the

Acceptable Use of Artificial Intelligence Policies may also be a helpful resource to consult.)

Strategies for Accessibility and DEI Evaluation

1. **Cost-Benefit Analysis:** Evaluate the cost of the AI tool against its potential benefits and impact on student learning outcomes. Consider long-term costs and the value it adds to the course. Consider what an achievable cost to a student is.
2. **Accessibility and Inclusivity:** Check if the AI tool is accessible to all students, including those with disabilities. Consider its usability for diverse learning styles and needs.
   a. Accessibility Features: Assess the AI tool's accessibility features, such as support for different languages, text-to-speech options, closed captioning, and adjustable font sizes. These features are essential for accommodating diverse learning needs.
   b. User Interface Design: Ensure that the AI tool's user interface is designed with inclusivity in mind. It should be intuitive and easy to navigate for all students, including those with disabilities.
3. **Representation and Bias:** Due to the inherent biases in much of the training data used by LLMs (Bender et al., 2021) most AI tools will have some bias. The following are some steps you might take to mitigate the associated risks:
   a. **Transparency of Sources:** Evaluate the degree to which the tool makes the sources of its training data known, and if the data is properly attributed n its results.
   b. **Inclusive Content:** Check if the AI tool offers content that reflects diverse cultures, experiences, and identities. It should cater to students from various backgrounds and not exclude or marginalize any group.
   c. **Language and Communication:** Verify that the AI tool can accurately understand and respond to diverse accents and communication styles to avoid excluding certain students.
   d. **Cultural Sensitivity:** Assess whether the AI tool demonstrates cultural sensitivity and avoids using content or examples that might be offensive or inappropriate for certain cultural groups.
4. **Alignment with DEI Initiatives:** Ensure that the adoption of the AI tool aligns with the institution's broader DEI initiatives and commitment to creating an inclusive learning environment.

Strategies for Student Input

When considering strategies for AI use in higher education, it's critical not to put the cart before the horse and craft usage policy that has significant implications for students without student input. A holistic approach that includes student input and involvement is paramount. Carving out space to ensure faculty are familiar with, involved, and respect the student users in all their plurality increases the chances that efforts are helping, not impeding students, while also giving some assurance that the practices and policies are crafted from an informed (as opposed to speculative) perspective, and therefore have greater potential to endure.

Institutions of higher education have to know their student bodies to the extent that their approach to AI and policy surrounding it bear their students in mind; and yet adhering to a standard, e.g. a SUNY-wide approach (not mandate) is just as important a litmus to draw out where a particular institution's students are in relation to an entire system. Thus, faculty and administration should be vigilant in their awareness of student AI usage, gathering qualitative and quantitative feedback that can continually be evaluated, assessed, and synthesized into respectable, relevant, and flexible policy while also preparing students for a world with AI. According to Veera Krohonen (2024), a research expert covering United States data for society, "a 2023 survey in the United States, [revealed that] 85% of undergraduate students would feel more comfortable using AI tools if they were developed and vetted by trusted academic sources." As educators in higher education, as we draft policy, we still need to remain cognizant of the fact that many students are already immersed in the world of AI and are waiting for us to catch up.

Once the dust (excitement, confusion, repulsion, narrative, and myth-making) begins to settle, more deliberate strategies for gathering student input will begin to surface (Walter, 2024). Regular, voluntary, and anonymous surveying, in whatever form, be it in-person or digital, remains a dependable approach. Utilizing QR code-linked surveys to catch students in passing on their phones may result in a higher yield of (and potentially more accurate) responses, given the familiarity and personal nature of the medium. These links can be deployed in focused environments like classrooms, class LMS pages, or in more communal spaces such as the library, student union, dormitories, or the college website. The library specifically is a prime location as the work of information literacy [read: AI literacy] falls directly in its wheelhouse. Given their open, communal settings and the relationships that are often formed therein between students, faculty, and librarians (also faculty), the likelihood of more candid and in-depth responses to the survey questions raises the potential for greater "statistical power, credibility, and generalizability" (Fass-Holmes, 2022).

Aside from open and honest classroom discussion of AI use, as well as instruction around ethical use of AI, which will soon be much more the norm, students should be surveyed broadly but concisely regarding: which AI tools they interface with and how, the quality of the output, and their perspective on how appropriately their professors and/or institution have or have not integrated AI into the classroom, with consideration given to how they anticipate it affecting their futures. This sample survey attempts to cover these key areas in an approachable 3-5 minute long survey that collects both qualitative and quantitative data. The survey tool automatically synthesizes data into digestible, reportable data sets, which we can use to design courses, stay abreast of changes in specific degree areas, and observe how AI is being used in career fields.

Similarly, if building a campus-wide survey is not doable, a way to build smaller sample size surveys while yielding important feedback regarding student use of AI is to center a survey inside an instructor's course. In-class surveys yield better answers than a survey disseminated by an unknown source and, as a bonus, help faculty learn about their students. Keeping surveys anonymous removes the fear students may feel regarding their answers impacting their class grades. In-class surveys have the potential to produce honest answers from students, especially if instructor-student relationships have grown over a semester, and a survey helps students feel integral to the design of the learning. Biesta and Stengal (2016), in "Thinking Philosophically About Teaching," refer to the relationship between teacher and student as partners in the process of questioning, and there are innumerable questions to ask about the use of AI in higher education (p. 15). Additionally, reciprocal sharing versus a top-down power structure creates a stronger course and one that reflects the interests of students, thereby correlating to greater student success (Freire, 1968). "Voices Inside Schools" by Carol R. Rodgers (2002) speaks to the sharing that is important in the classroom, "I encourage teachers to value student feedback as critical to understanding students' learning . . . most teachers rarely take the time to engage their students in conversations about their learning" (p. 233). A survey allows a teacher to be a learner and look at the subject matter through the eyes of their students (Rogers, 2002, p. 243).

Surveys in the classroom allow professors to make evidence-based decisions to adjust teaching practices such as incorporating AI. If a survey shows what AI tools students engage with, they can then work to build content to help them use AI tools responsibly. A survey has the added benefit of being a professional development tool as it encourages instructors to engage and grow in their field on an ongoing basis. In the article "Improving Teaching With Expert Feedback—From Students" (2016), information acquired from a survey improves a professor's effectiveness, and the classroom remains student-centered. "By listening to their students, educators can continuously evolve and enhance their teaching practices". As we work towards reciprocal relationships with our students and learn what AI will look like in the classroom, we must also remain focused on protecting our students' identities and teaching them how to do the same.

Preparing students for life after college requires that we adequately equip them for the workplace and a broader audience. Keeping abreast of the ever-changing landscape of AI is our professional and ethical responsibility, allowing us to help our students reach their long-term goals of economic and upward mobility and future readiness in the workplace. As we build relationships between university curricula and careers, it is important we also teach them how to protect their identities, as we have a professional obligation to safeguard student data privacy. For example, all personal information must be omitted to comply with the Family Educational Rights and Privacy Act (FERPA). Additionally, we must "think of AI Chatbots as public data warehouses," so as you incorporate AI into your classroom, Copilot, a Microsoft AI tool, recommends the following:

- Understand that the data you enter into an AI chatbot may be stored by the company running the tool.
- Companies use this data for training future models, potentially including user-submitted information.
- Even if anonymized, there's always a risk of data breaches. (Open AI, 2024)

Teaching our students to be careful with personal information by removing specific identifiers is a part of helping our students to be safe with their personal information when they move beyond our classrooms. For instance, using Copilot instead of ChatGPT allows the user to know where Copilot is pulling information as they share their sources with the user. This added benefit allows us to work with our students on checking the credibility of the sources from which Copilot pulled information. This is an important tool to build a student's information literacy skills and is part of the SUNY General Education Framework implemented in Fall 2023.

Certainly, if we are considering using survey data for research publication, it becomes critical to protect ourselves and our students through institutional support and the institutional review board that comes with it. Additionally, awareness of the timing of the surveys as it relates to the broader institutional and discipline-specific surveying calendar, as well as student survey fatigue, is important (Fass-Holmes, 2022).

A Statista survey (2024) revealed that "65% of students also believe that AI will improve how they learn, rather than having negative consequences on learning." If we are to take anything away from this statistic, it is that, as educators, we have an obligation to help guide our students through the unchartered waters of AI. If we embrace where we are with AI, rather than look at the use of AI through a punitive lens, the possibilities of change in higher education due to AI are not to be feared but rather a journey to share with students.

PART VI
SPECIAL SECTION: A BRIEF HISTORY OF AI

For thousands of years there has been the notion of a thinking automaton, or machine, such as the bronze man Talos from the Argonautica (3 BC) or the golems in the Talmud. As technology advanced, developing machines that appear intelligent or on their own volition began to appear. By 1764 the Canard Digérateur (digesting duck) was built; the duck would quack, muddle water with its bill, eat grain pellets and later poop them out (Wood, 2003). The claim that it digested the food was later revealed to be a clever trick, and not actual digestion. Much like the Schachtürke (Mechanical Turk) that purported to be a master chess playing automaton (Levitt, 2000), the Canard Digérateur was an impressive mechanism whose designers intended to fool others about its actual abilities. With a history of deception with 'thinking machines', as well as the development of computers, it might seem surprising that Alan Turing (1950) proposed a test to judge machine intelligence on whether it can fool us into thinking it is a person. Nevertheless, by 1950 computers could store and execute commands, albeit it was vastly expensive to do so (Williams, 1997). Technology was enabling computing machinery that could not otherwise be built before.

In 1956 Dartmouth College coined the term "Artificial Intelligence" during a summer research conference organized by John McCarthy. Allen Newell, Herbert Simon, and Cliff Shaw attended and demonstrated Logic Theorist (1956), a program using a virtual problem solver using heuristics to solve mathematical theorems similar to those in Principia Mathematica by Whitehead and Russell (1910). Prior to this point, computers did not use heuristic programming. Logic Theorist is arguably the first AI program. Its success inspired Newell and Simon to develop General Problem Solver (1959) and ushered in a golden era of research in AI.

Inspired by biological models of neural networks by Warren McCullock (1943), John Rosenblatt developed an electronic device with the capability to learn and called it a 'perceptron' in 1958. These networks excelled at pattern recognition. However, in 1969 Minsky and Papert critiqued the effectiveness of a two-level network for learning which thwarted its success despite Rosenblatt proposing a multi-level network (more than two). The debate between analytical AI and proponents of neural networks continued for years.

The general success of AI that followed is aptly reflected by a Minsky quote from Life magazine, "From three to eight years we will have a machine with the intelligence of a human being" (Darrach,1970). Research began to hit a wall however, and less money was being invested in AI. The idea of using terms such as 'thinking' or 'intelligence' became out of style following McDurmott's criticism of the misuse of these terms in his paper "Artificial Intelligence Meets Natural Stupidity" (1976). As complex problems challenged the technical limits with vast search spaces, researchers focused more on problems with a well-defined scope and referred to the work as 'applied artificial intelligence'.

A shift in AI programming occurred to focus on knowledge gathered from experts. Edward Feigenbaum's work developed some of the first 'expert systems' that proved successful at tasks such as identifying compounds from spectral readings (Buchanan & Feigenbaum, 1978). By restricting the search domain to a narrow scope, such as specific knowledge that could be acquired from real-world experts on a given topic, the machines could manage the search domain and successfully find answers. The systems could then be used by non-experts to assist them. This was the first time these systems could be directly applied in industries.

Japan's Fifth Generation Computing initiative provided a significant source of funding for massively parallel and concurrent logic systems (Shapiro, 1983). The attention helped revive interest in connectionist architectures (neural networks). During this time, "deep learning" techniques became more popular (Rumelhart & McClelland, 1987) and analytic tools progressed. For example, adding multiple layers to networks and employing feedback proved fecund and eventually was applied to optical character recognition (Russell & Norvig, 2003). Likewise, developments in a gradient estimation method, called "backpropagation" (Devaney, 1982), used to train neural networks began to produce significant results (Rumelhart et al., 1986). Backpropagation is still used today in many areas, such as speech recognition and language processing (Janciauskas & Chang, 2018). Its efficiency also assists with Sophia, a phonetic processor at Stanford (Liu et al., 2024).

With developments in the internet, massive complex datasets, or "big data", allowed for a fecund synergy with neural networks. Deep learning machines required large datasets. Big data was beginning to fulfill this need. Meanwhile, Moore's law, i.e., the growth of microprocessors is exponential (Moore, 1965), allowed for computing power to rapidly grow over the next decade. The advances in graphics cards or graphics processing units (GPUs), also began to contribute to the success in image detection. Even with the success, researchers were leery of using the moniker "AI" given its connotations of failed promises and science fiction references (Markoff, 2005).

The ImageNet competition in 2012 was a great step for deep learning. Just two years earlier, a breakthrough in deep learning occurred when work revealed that neural networks can perform unsupervised handwriting recognition using backpropagation (Ciresan et al., 2010). During the competition, AlexNet achieved a 15.3% error rate using convolutional neural network, a type of feed-forward neural network that regulates certain gradients when using backpropagation (Krizhevsky et al., 2012). This was over 10% better than all prior attempts. Part of their success was to heavily rely on GPUs. The success sparked massive work on image recognition and produced networks with a 95% accuracy rate by 2017 (Gershgorn, 2017). Besides image recognition, generative adversarial networks were showing promise at generating new results (Goodfellow et al., 2014). Underlying this success is the access to a massive amount of computing machines. A 'modest' network will contain only 2000 CPUs working together (Dean et al., 2012).

By 2016, natural language processing models were trained on a single domain of text, such as news articles (Jozefowicz et al., 2016). Training on a wide range of data sets across multiple domains was recommended to increase success (Radford et al., 2018). Large language models (LLMs), or vast neural networks used for classification and natural language processing, focused on statistical relationships between text documents. They frequently used self-supervised learning, which then began to demonstrate success. By 2022, ChatGPT jettisoned AI into the public eye. While a novelty at first, successful prompt engineering can generate very useful outputs (Lock, 2022). OpenAI followed by releasing multi-modal improvements with GPT-4 (Wiggers, 2023). Meanwhile, several other LLMs have been released or are in development, such as Google's PaLM or Meta's LLaMA. It is important to recognize that the computational requirements of LLMs are exponentially greater than previous neural networks; GPT3, for example, required 285,000 CPU cores and 10,000 GPUs to train it (Tauscher, 2020).

Currently, AI seems ubiquitous in the media and it should raise some serious questions. First, is it really accomplishing what it claims? It is not clear if we are ascribing intentionality to AI chatbots that are stochastic parrots generating text without a clue to its meaning (Bender et al., 2021). To date, it is clear that most AI chatbots do not understand the context of questions or the social appropriateness of their generated answers. For example, AI Playground suggested that an Asian graduate student should change her LinkedIn profile photo to a Caucasian image to look more professional (Singh, 2023). Relying on AI for decisions that can affect lives can be dangerous and currently there is an estimated $75 billion invested in AI (Amdur, 2023). This can greatly incentivize unscrupulous behavior.

Much like the Schachtürke (Mechanical Turk), the AI tools may appear to provide a service disingenuously. To circumvent these options and to protect people from potential dangers that these mistakes may incur, we need to remember that understanding the architecture is critical. By better understanding these tools and their effects on our lives, we can employ them more ethically. We can benefit from these tools while ensuring their ethical and responsible applications.

PART VI
CONCLUSION

What Does the Future with AI Look Like?

AI's increasing ability to process larger and larger amounts of data and to analyze it with increasingly sophisticated algorithms is likely to result in improvements in all areas. Determining the future with precision, though, is more difficult. It will depend on several factors, not the least of which are the regulations that are developed now and how they are enforced.

These examples may give us a taste of what the future might bring, plus a few that might tickle your imagination.

Job Market

It's routinely recognized that AI will impact jobs in the near and more distant future. Not only is it predicted that AI will result in job cuts this year (Fleming, 2024), but there are predictions that in the long run more than 300 million jobs will be lost or downgraded (Kelly, 2023). However, new skills will also be needed and new jobs created. Change brings opportunity as well. Did you know that "human alarm clock" was once a job? Called "knocker-uppers" (Peek, 2016), they walked the streets tapping on windows with a long stick to wake people up for work. The Future of Jobs Report 2023 (World Economic Forum, 2023) suggests that job creation will occur especially in the fields of "AI and machine learning specialists, data analysts and scientists, and digital transformation specialists".

Scientific Discovery

Scientific discovery is the basis of progress in so many fields, and AI is destined to play a big role. For example, Harvard Medical School has developed the technology to predict the evolution of a virus (Willige, 2023). Imagine if that had been available before the pandemic struck. Now imagine the future.

Another example has to do with identifying protein structure. Proteins are essential to supporting our lives and understanding their structure is central. Alphabet – Google's new AlphaFold – is reported to have predicted the structure of all known proteins, and is ready to make significant progress. This information will be used to discover new diseases, new drugs, and new vaccines.

Then there's the goal of personalized medicine, seen as a major milestone in healthcare. AI could prove to be the vector for developing personalized treatment in a much shorter period of time, including omitting the need for clinical trials (Tewari, 2022). Finally, review of existing scientific research is important in the development of new research (Schmidt, 2023). This is another way that AI could play a significant role.

Cyber Security

Cyber attacks, which have steadily increased, are up 20% in the last year and are now at their highest ever

(Madnick, 2023). According to the Harvard Business Review (Madnick, 2024), globally the number of victims doubled in the past year.

AI, in its ability to crunch large amounts of live data, analyze it in real-time, and make predictions, is becoming a major player in cyber defense. The size and scope of its abilities can be used proactively to discover vulnerabilities and trigger automatic responses. The same strengths applied to dynamic threat detection work to identify anomalies as well as indicate false positives. Further, AI can be used to train people who work with AI. The effectiveness of AI will depend on many things, not the least of which is the scope and accuracy of its data set, which will need constant updating.

The same capabilities are unfortunately available to generate threatening attacks. In just one example of many reported by the Center for Strategic and International Studies (CSIS) (n.d.) to have occurred in January of this year, webcams in Kyiv were hacked to glean information on the city's air defense system before a missile attack was launched.

AI is seen to play a significant role in the physical as well as the digital battlefield. Benjamin Jensen, speaking before the U.S. Senate Select Committee about national security ("Addressing the National Security Implications of AI", 2023), pointed out that enlisted men in the military will need training in data science and coding in order to respond to the rapidly changing information supplied by AI in the dynamic environment of the battlefield. He observed that "The general or spy who doesn't have a model by their side in the 21st century will be blind man in a bar fight."

Does all this augur defense without human intervention? Not so. Mr. Jensen is not the only one who believes its strength is within the hands of human beings. Human control and insight is, in fact, recommended throughout the industry (Avey, 2023).

Here are a few future possibilities that may be a little harder to predict:

AI and Mindreading

There is research showing that AI can be used to read thoughts (Tang et al., 2023). Brain activity was recorded through a cap that registered electrical activity; then AI was used to convert it into intelligible text. Neural decoding is not new, but recent research has been made public. The value of this technology can be inestimable for people with communication difficulties. It also, however, raises questions: Where will it stop? In the future, will a cap be necessary? Will wireless technology do the job? …. In the long run, what will happen to privacy?

If you have not heard enough, let us share one more apparently far-fetched thought. Leo Kim in Wired Magazine (2023) posits the idea that this technology, not unlike others, could be reversed. Will there come a time when technology could, in fact, change our thoughts?

Interspecies Communication

Doctor Dolittle may have had it right — with the help of generative AI. We've been making efforts over the years to understand animals with some success. With the help of generative AI, we may be able to accomplish this more fully and more quickly (Love et al., 2024). What about the reverse? Once we decode their language, it's not that far to believe we could communicate it back to them and establish two-way communication. (If you're interested in seeing moving elephants up close and in hearing some of their communication, check out "How AI is decoding the animal kingdom".)

After Death Communication (in a way)

Using hours of recorded conversation with a person before their death, generative AI has been used to converse with them, even ask their advice, afterward (Carballo, 2023). There are various tools, some as simple as a laptop in their home, that can be used to capture what the person has to share. Some people are not comfortable with the results, others are elated by the experience.

AI is here. Fasten your seatbelt!

Appendix A: Timeline

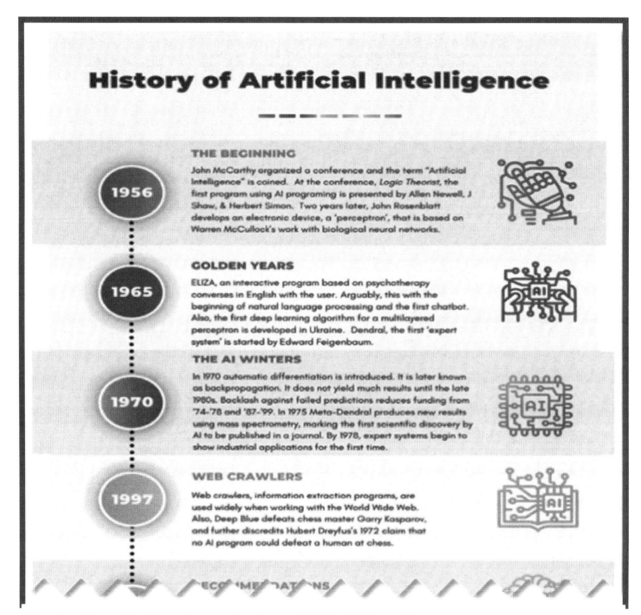

A Timeline of Some Significant Events in the History of AI: 1950-2000 (part 1)

History of Artificial Intelligence

1956 — THE BEGINNING
John McCarthy organized a conference and the term "Artificial Intelligence" is coined. At the conference, *Logic Theorist*, the first program using AI programing is presented by Allen Newell, J Shaw, & Herbert Simon. Two years later, John Rosenblatt develops an electronic device, a 'perceptron', that is based on Warren McCullock's work with biological neural networks.

2005 — RECOMMENDATIONS
AI programs using web tracking activity and media use offer recommendations and are used for marketing. Four years later a recurrent neural network wins three handwriting recognition contests.

2014 — IMAGE & LANGUAGE RECOGNITION
AlexNet, a deep learning model, wins the ImageNet competition with a significantly better error rate than anything before. In three years, image recognition networks become 95% efficient. Meanwhile, personal assistants using natural language processing are standard of most smartphones.

2020 — LARGE LANGUAGE MODELS
OpenAI introduces GPT-3, a large language model that uses deep learning to produce various outputs. In two years, ChatGPT, an AI chatbot with a browser interface, using the GPT-3.5 LLM is released for the public to use. Today various AI tools are available on the web.

A Timeline of Some Significant Events in the History of AI: 2000-Present (part 2)

Appendix B: Algorithmic/Machine-Learning Bias

Machine Learning Bias

There are several types of machine bias. A few of the more common types include:

Association Bias

This bias misleads the learning process when an association occurs from a bias in the training data. When this data is collected, it is often reinforced by cultural biases. For example, many women who play video games online opt for accounts that suggest they are male to avoid online harassment. If an algorithm is trained by a dataset based on account monikers, it will bias the algorithm to suggest fewer women play video games online; this effectively yields a result that also confirms a cultural bias.

Emergent Bias

This bias is a result of applying the algorithm to new data or contexts. If the training data is aligned to hypothetical datasets instead of real-world contexts, the bias results in overlooking key features that would otherwise dismiss the spurious or inappropriate correlation. The bias can be further exacerbated by feedback loops that confirm the bias with new data that confirms the correlation. For example, the Correctional Offender Management Profiling for Alternative Sanctions (COMPAS) algorithm, which was employed by several states, extracted data from arrests and used this data to predict the likelihood to of individuals to commit crimes by effectively adopting racial profiling and racial bias accelerated by the feedback loop (Angwin et al., 2016). COMPAS modeled the common bias already known, and not desired, in arrest statistics. (Carson, 2021).

Exclusion Bias

This occurs when the modelers fail to recognize the importance of a data point that would otherwise consequently influence the training. By excluding the data, the training is significantly altered and thus displays the bias.

Language Bias

Statistical sampling frequently uses data from English-language sources. This can distort training in large language models to ignore non-English language groups and distort topics more familiar to their culture (Luo, et. al, 2023).

Marginalized Bias

Traditionally under-represented or marginalized groups are not adequately included in training sets which creates a direct bias. These groups include bias against race, gender, sexual orientation, political affiliation, and disability. For example, when datasets over-represented Caucasians, darker skinned pedestrians were less safe self-driving cars trained by these datasets (Wilson, et al., 2019).

Measurement Bias

Underlying problems with the accuracy of the data and the process of how it was measured corrupt the training. Simply, invalid measurements or data collection methods will create measurement bias and biased output. For example, hospitals might judge high-risk patients based on their previous use of the health care system but not include the variability of health care accessibility for some populations (Cook, n.d.).

Recall Bias

Just before training, labels are inconsistently applied to the data based on subjective observation from the trainers, creating a false-positive rate. Since the data recalled is not precise for training, these estimation values create a bias or variance from the true values.

Sample Bias

This occurs when the data used for training is too small, or not a representative sample to accurately train the algorithm. An example of this would be training a neural network about college faculty while only using photos of elderly white men who are faculty.

Examples of Algorithmic Bias

When not accounted for, algorithmic bias can create great harm. Often the victims of the bias are the same victims of societal prejudice. A few of these cases include:

Amazon Automated Hiring

In 2014 Amazon began engineering an algorithm to automate hiring; by 2018 its algorithm demonstrated a marginalized bias (sex-bias). Amazon's software engineers skewed disproportionately male. When using the existing pool of employees as training data, the algorithm naturally downgraded resumes with references to 'women's' and graduates of two all-women; s colleges. (Dastin, 2018). Amazon tried correcting these issues, but the bias continued and then discontinued the program in 2018 (Goodman, 2018).

Medical Industry

In 2007 the Vaginal Birth after Cesarean Delivery (VBAC) algorithm was designed for providers to assess the safety of giving birth vaginally for their patients, and illuminating women at risk of uterine ruptures. While the training data focused on factors such as the woman's age, it predicted that Black and Hispanic women were less likely to have a successful vaginal birth after having a C-section than non-Hispanic white women. Effectively, the algorithm identified symptoms of inequality based on instructional racism and attributed these as medical factors to guide prognosis. In 2017, research revealed that error and that it caused doctors to perform more C-sections on these on Black and Hispanic women than on non-Hispanic white women (Vas et al., 2019). While few large-scale deployments of AI currently exist, the above issue demonstrates just one of the concerns of its application (Panch et al., 2019). Moreover, most positive results from AI systems using patient data are fraught with issues (Fraser et al., 2018). Regardless, we can expect a growing reliance on AI in healthcare (Mittermaier et al., 2023)

Mortgage Lending

Credit scores have a long history of intentional and legalized discrimination that still display racial bias (Wu, 2024), however AI bias has amplified the effects when an algorithm was applied to mortgage lending. Compared to white applicants, lenders were; 40% more likely to turn down Latino applicants, 50% more likely to turn down Asian/Pacific Islander applicants; 70% more likely to turn down Native American applicants, even if all candidates met the same criteria (Martinez and Kirchner, 2021). Further, 80% of black mortgage applicants were denied (Hale, 2021). By adopting seemingly non-partial algorithms to large data sets, the AI bias has contributed to institutional racism that will probably create more data about homeownership rates that can be used to perpetuate its bias.

Appendix C: AI Tool Evaluation Examples

Examples of evaluating potential AI tools for implementation in higher education

Example A: Midjourney

A review of Midjourney, a generative AI text-to-picture program that allows users to create images based off of prompts. This AI tool was evaluated using all three considerations lists (e.g., pedagogy, technology, as well as accessibility & DEI.

Midjourney Draft Review

Example B: Almanack.ai

A review of Almanack.ai, a "smart course material generator and lesson planner for educators" (Almanack.ai, 2023). This AI tool was evaluated using all three consideration lists (e.g., pedagogy, technology, as well as accessibility & DEI).

Almanack AI.docx

Example C: Learnt.ai

A review of Learnt.ai, which can help save time and effort by automating the creation of lesson plans, learning objectives, assessment questions, and a range of other resources. Learnt.ai is designed to augment not replace, to inspire instructors to create engaging content that aligns with best practices in education, making it easier to deliver effective and impactful lessons to students (Learnt.ai, 2023).

Learnt.AI Draft Review

Appendix D: Glossary

AI

Artificial intelligence leverages computers and machines to attempt to mimic the problem-solving and decision-making capabilities of the human mind.

Tasks may require human abilities such as perception, reasoning, problem solving, and understanding natural language. Large collections of data as well as new experiences are used by algorithms to find patterns and use them to take actions or make predictions/provide insights (IBM, 2023).

AI Forensics

This refers to the use of forensic techniques to identify if text was AI-generated and then the source of the AI product. Once the source is known, it can be checked for accuracy and credits. This can ultimately reveal the bias in the training data set (Martineau, 2023).

Algorithm

A set of step-by-step directions for solving a problem or accomplishing a specific task (Berkman Klein Center, 2019).

As an example, here's a simple computer algorithm for finding the highest number in a list:

1. Start with the first number in the list and remember it as the current, most significant number.
2. Compare the current largest number with the next number in the list.
3. If the next number is larger than the current most significant number, update the current largest number to be the next number.
4. Repeat steps 2 and 3 for all the numbers in the list.
5. When you reach the end of the list, the current largest number will be the largest number in the list.

Deep Learning

A subset of machine learning using a neural network with at least three layers. Deep learning distinguishes itself from classical machine learning by the type of data that it works with and the methods in which it learns.

Machine learning algorithms leverage structured, labeled data to make predictions—meaning that specific features are defined from the input data for the model and organized into tables; there is generally some pre-processing to organize the data into a structured format.

Deep learning eliminates some of data pre-processing that is typically involved with machine learning. These algorithms can ingest and process unstructured data, like text and images, and it automates feature extraction, removing some of the dependency on human experts. For example, let's say that we had a set of photos of different pets, and we wanted to categorize them by "cat", "dog", "hamster", et cetera. Deep learning algorithms can determine which features (e.g. ears) are most important to distinguish each animal from another. In machine learning, this hierarchy of features is established manually by a human expert" (IBM, n.d.).

Deepfake

Deepfakes are digital forgeries that use artificial intelligence to create believable but misleading images, audio, and videos (Personal and Security Research Center, 2022).

Generative AI

Generative AI is a type of AI system capable of generating text, images, or other media in response to prompts. It uses its collection of data and experiences to generate new content. Generative AI is different from General AI (see below) (Benefits and Limitations, 2023).

General AI / Artificial General Intelligence (AGI)

General AI refers to the development of AI systems that possess human-level intelligence across a broad range of tasks and domains. AGI aims to create machines that can understand, learn, and perform complex cognitive functions that mimic human intelligence. This is in comparison to the specific, task-focused output of Generative AI (Mock, 2023).

Hallucinations

Since generative AI is based on statistical patterns, it may not always produce accurate or meaningful results. "Hallucinations" refers to computer-generated information that does not correspond to objective reality (Mair, 2023; Alkasissi & McFarlane, 2023).

Large Language Model (LLM)

A deep learning algorithm that can recognize, summarize, translate, predict and generate text and other forms of content based on knowledge gained from massive datasets (Lee, 2023).

Machine Learning

A subfield of AI where a computer imitates human learning using data and algorithms to gradually improve its accuracy without additional programming changes or corrections (IBM, n.d.; Brown, 2021).

Model

A program that is trained on a dataset to identify patterns and, possibly, make decisions (IBM, n.d.). In machine learning, algorithms that go through training develop an understanding of a topic, or their own "model" of the world.

Multimodality

The ability of generative AI to provide responses based on multiple types of prompting material that can include images, audio, and possible others, as well as text (Infusion, 2023).

Natural Language Processing (NLP)

A branch of artificial intelligence that enables understanding and production of human language by a computer (IBM, n.d.). It became popular in smart speakers like Siri and Alexa.

Neural Network

Mathematical models for programming inspired by the human brain, primarily for problem solving and pattern recognition. These can be fairly simple or include multiple internal layers meant to increase learning capacity, efficiency, and accuracy (Zwass, 2023). Data fed to a neural network is reduced into smaller pieces and analyzed for underlying patterns, often from thousands to millions of times depending on the complexity of the network. A deep neural network is when the output of one neural network is fed into the input of another, chaining them together as layers. Various types of neural networks include:

- Convolutional Neural Network (CNN): A neural network with the ability to process dense data, such as millions of pixels or tens of thousands of audio samples. These networks are primarily used to recognize images, video, and audio data. They are effective for learning with less parameters, however are comparatively slow and complex to maintain.
- Deep Neural Network: A neural network that contains more than one hidden layer, i.e., layers between the input and output layers.
- Generative Adversarial Network (GAN): A system in which two neural networks, one that generates an output and another that checks the quality of that output against what it should look like. For example, when attempting to generate a picture of a cat, the generator will create an image, and the other network (called a discriminator) will make the generator try again if it fails to recognize a cat in the image.
- Recurrent Neural Network (RNN): A neural network frequently employed for natural language processing. It analyzes data cyclically and sequentially, i.e., it can process data such as sentences or words while maintaining their order and context in a sentence.
- Long Short-Term Memory Network (LSTM): A variation of a recurrent neural network that is intended to retain structured information based on data. An RNN could recognize all the nouns and adjectives in a sentence and if they're used correctly, but an LSTM could remember its placement in a book.

Prompt

Prompts are the requests/information we provide to AI to let it know what we're looking for. They may be snippets of text, streams of speech, or blocks of pixels in a still image or video. The importance of an effective prompt has generated a new job – **Prompt Engineer**. (Martineau, 2023; Popli, 2023; Shieh, 2023).

Prompt Injection Attack

A prompt injection attack crafts a prompt that causes the AI tool to provide output that has been forbidden by its training (Selvi, 2022).

Puppeteering

Puppeteering refers to the manipulation of full-body images to perform actions and behaviors determined by AI (like a puppeteer). It is also known as full body deepfakes. For example, the image of someone who has two left feet when it comes to dancing could be made to perform as if they were a talented dancer (Jaiman, 2022).

Training

The process of supplying data (usually data sets) to an algorithm for it to learn. It can apply to various machine architectures, or models, including neural networks. Three styles of machine learning training include:

- Supervised Learning: The data fed to the algorithm to process is already organized and labeled. The goal of most supervised learning is to predict output based on known input. For example, if you are training a network with supervised learning to identify cars by providing the model with thousands of images labeled "cars". The approach helps minimize error between the outputs and the actual images. Common techniques of supervised learning include: linear regression, logical regression and decision trees.
- Unsupervised Learning: The algorithm is not provided any information about how it should categorize the data it is given, but instead it must find relationships and classify the unlabeled data. The goal of employing this style of learning is to identify valuable relationships between input data points. These relationships can then be applied to new input. This approach finds spatters, anomalies, and similarities within the data. Common techniques include: clustering, probability density, and associated rule learning.
- Self-Supervised Learning: The algorithm uses the structure within the data, its own inputs or modifications, to generate labels. Self-supervised learning typically identifies a secondary task where

labels can be automatically obtained, and then trains the network on the secondary task. While the targets are missing in both unsupervised learning and self-supervised learning, the latter uses the data itself to generate the supervisory signals.

References

Abdallah, M., & Salah, M. (2024). Artificial intelligence and intellectual properties: Legal and ethical considerations. *International Journal of Intelligent Systems and Applications in Engineering, 12*(1), 368-376. Retrieved from https://ijisae.org/index.php/IJISAE/article/view/3911

Abdous, M. (2023, March 21). *How AI is shaping the future of higher ed.* Inside Higher Ed. https://www.insidehighered.com/views/2023/03/22/how-ai-shaping-future-higher-ed-opinion

Academic honesty and integrity: What should a syllabus statement on AI look like? Colorado State University. Retrieved July 27, 2023, from https://tilt.colostate.edu/what-should-a-syllabus-statement-on-ai-look-like/

Addressing the National Security Implications of AI, (2023). https://www.csis.org/analysis/addressing-national-security-implications-ai

Alchemy. [Danny Liu]. (2023, August 3). *Harnessing the power of AI: Transforming assignments and assessments in higher education* [Video]. YouTube. https://www.youtube.com/watch?v=y5As7zVDzRQ

Alizadeh, H., Sharifi, A., Damanbagh, S., Nazarnia, H., & Nazarnia, M. (2023). Impacts of the COVID-19 pandemic on the social sphere and lessons for crisis management: a literature review. *Nat Hazards 117*, 2139–2164. https://doi.org/10.1007/s11069-023-05959-2

Alkaissi, H., & McFarlane, S. I. (2023). Artificial hallucinations in ChatGPT: Implications in scientific writing. *Cureus, 15*(2), e35179. https://doi.org/10.7759/cureus.35179

Alqahtani, T., Badreldin, H. A., Alrashed, M., Alshaya, A. I., Alghamdi, S. S., bin Saleh, K., Alowais, S. A., Alshaya, O. A., Rahman, I., Al Yami, M. S., & Albekairy, A. M. (2023). The emergent role of artificial intelligence, natural learning processing, and large language models in higher education and research. *Research in Social and Administrative Pharmacy, 19*(8). https://doi.org/10.1016/j.sapharm.2023.05.016

Alston, S. (2023, March 6). *How generative AI is being used to enhance accessibility and inclusion for people with disabilities.* LinkedIn. https://www.linkedin.com/pulse/how-generative-ai-being-used-enhance-accessibility-inclusion-alston/

Altman, S. (2023, May 16). Written testimony of sam altman chief executive officer openai before the U.S. Senate committee on the judiciary subcommittee on privacy, technology, & the law. *Sam Written Testimony Draft – Senate Hearing.* https://www.judiciary.senate.gov/imo/media/doc/2023-05-16%20-%20Bio%20&%20Testimony%20-%20Altman.pdf

Amatriain, X. (2024, February 8). *Prompt design and engineering: Introduction and advanced methods.* ArXiv.org. https://doi.org/10.48550/arXiv.2401.14423

Amdur, Eli. (2023 Nov 16). Venture capital in AI – Where and how much. *Forbes.* Retrieved April 10, 20204 from https://www.forbes.com/sites/eliamdur/2023/11/16/venture-capital-in-ai--where-and-how-much/?sh=602413ee20e0

Antonacci, M. & Maize, M. (2023). Physics writing in the era of Artificial Intelligence. *American Journal of Physics. 91*(8). 575. https://pubs.aip.org/aapt/ajp/article/91/8/575/2902649/Physics-writing-in-the-era-of-artificial

Appel, G., Neelbauer, J., & Schweidel, D. (2023, April 07). Generative AI has an intellectual property problem. *Harvard Business Review.* Retrieved March 19, 2024 from https://hbr.org/2023/04/generative-ai-has-an-intellectual-property-problem

Artificial Intelligence (AI). (n.d.) *Nature Portfolio.* Retrieved March 11, 2024, from https://www.nature.com/nature-portfolio/editorial-policies/ai

Avey, C. (2023, October 4). *The future of cybersecurity in an AI-driven world*. IEEE Computer Society. https://www.computer.org/publications/tech-news/trends/cybersecurity-in-an-ai-driven-world

Bano, M., Zowghi, D., Shea, P., & Ibarra, G. (2023). *Investigating responsible AI for scientific research: An empirical study*. arxiv.org. https://arxiv.org/ftp/arxiv/papers/2312/2312.09561.pdf

Bender, E. M., Gebru, T., McMillan-Major, A., & Shmitchell, S. (2021). On the dangers of stochastic parrots: Can language models be too big? 🦜. *Proceedings of the 2021 ACM Conference on Fairness, Accountability, and Transparency*, 610–623. https://doi.org/10.1145/3442188.3445922

Berkman Klein Center for Internet & Society. (2019, November). *What is an algorithm?* Digital Citizenship + Resource Platform. https://dcrp.berkman.harvard.edu/tool/what-algorithm

Briggs, J. & Kodnani, D. (2023, March 26). *The potentially large effects of artificial intelligence on economic growth*. Goldman Sachs Economic Research. https://www.gspublishing.com/content/research/en/reports/2023/03/27/d64e052b-0f6e-45d7-967b-d7be35fabd16.html

British Academy. (2021). *The COVID decade: Understanding the long-term societal impacts of COVID-19*. The British Academy, doi.org/10.5871/bac19stf/9780856726583.001

Britannica, T. Editors of Encyclopaedia (2024, March 13). higher education. Encyclopedia Britannica. https://www.britannica.com/topic/higher-educationBrown, J. (2023, February 22).

Brown, S. (2021, April 21). *Machine learning, explained*. MIT Management Sloan School. https://mitsloan.mit.edu/ideas-made-to-matter/machine-learning-explained

Bruff, D. (2023, July 13). *Assignment makeovers in the AI age: Reading response edition*. Agile Learning. Retrieved August 14, 2023, from https://derekbruff.org/?p=4083.

Bruff, D. (2023, July 19). *Assignment makeovers in the AI age: Essay edition*. Agile Learning. Retrieved August 14, 2023, from https://derekbruff.org/?p=4105.

Buchanan, B. & Feigenbaum, E. (1978). Dendral and meta-dendral: Their application dimension. *Artificial Intelligence*. 11(1-2), 5-24. https://www.sciencedirect.com/science/article/abs/pii/0004370278900103

Bushard, B. (2024, August). *AI-Generated Robocalls Banned After Troubling Deepfakes*. Forbes. https://www.forbes.com/sites/brianbushard/2024/02/08/ai-generated-robocalls-banned-after-troubling-deepfakes/?sh=28dec8f38cfa

Caira, C., Lusso, L., & Aranda, L. (2023, March 8). *Artificially Inequitable? AI and closing the gender gap*. OECD. AI Policy Observatory. Retrieved on March 15, 2024, from https://oecd.ai/en/wonk/closing-the-gender-gap

Calhoun, V. (2023, May 23). *The future of higher education – The rise of ChatGPT on your campus*. NASPA. https://www.naspa.org/blog/the-future-of-higher-education-the-rise-of-ai-and-chatgpt-on-your-campus

Carballo, R. (2023, December 11). *Using A.I. to talk to the dead*. The New York Times. https://www.nytimes.com/2023/12/11/technology/ai-chatbots-dead-relatives.html

Carless, D. & Boud, D. (2018). The development of student feedback literacy: Enabling uptake of feedback. *Assessment & Evaluation in Higher Education*, 43(8), 1315–1325. https://doi.org/10.1080/02602938.2018.1463354.

Cazzaniga et al. (2024). *Gen-AI: Artificial Intelligence and the Future of Work*. IMF Staff Discussion Note SDN2024/001, International Monetary Fund, Washington, DC.

Center for Strategic and International Studies. (n.d.). *Significant Cyber Incidents*. https://www.csis.org/programs/strategic-technologies-program/significant-cyber-incidents

Chechitelli, A. (2023, May 23). *AI writing detection update from Turnitin's chief product officer*. Turnitin. Retrieved August 14, 2023, from https://www.turnitin.com/blog/ai-writing-detection-update-from-turnitins-chief-product-officer

Chen, C. (2023, March 9). *AI Will Transform Teaching and Learning. Let's Get it Right*. Stanford University Human-Centered Artificial Intelligence. https://hai.stanford.edu/news/ai-will-transform-teaching-and-learning-lets-get-it-right

Chicago Manual of Style (n.d.). *Citation, documentation of sources*. Retrieved August 10, 2023, from https://www.chicagomanualofstyle.org/qanda/data/faq/topics/Documentation/faq0422.html

Chopra, R., Clarke, K., Burrows, C.A, & Khan, L.M. (2023, April). *Joint Statement on*

Enforcement Efforts Against Discrimination and Bias in Automated Systems. US Equal Employment Opportunity Commission. https://www.eeoc.gov/joint-statement-enforcement-efforts-against-discrimination-and-bias-automated-systems

Ciresan, D., Meier, U.,Gambardella, L., & Schmidhuber, J. (2010). Deep big simple neural nets for handwritten digit recognition. *Neural Computation, 22*(12), 3207-3220. https://arxiv.org/abs/1003.0358

Cohen, M. (2023, June 1). *Here's how A.I.-backed tools can help with worker stress and mental health*. CNBC Technology Executive Council. https://www.cnbc.com/2023/06/01/heres-how-ai-backed-tools-can-help-worker-stress-and-mental-health.html

Cook, A. (n.d.). Identifying Bias in AI [Online Course]. Kaggle. https://www.kaggle.com/code/alexisbcook/identifying-bias-in-ai

Cowls, J., Tsamados, A., Taddeo, M., & Floridi, L. (2021). The AI gambit: leveraging artificial intelligence to combat climate change—opportunities, challenges, and recommendations. *AI & Society, 38*(1), 283–307. https://doi.org/10.1007/s00146-021-01294-x

Crabtree, M. (2024). *What is Prompt Engineering? A Detailed Guide For 2024*. Data Camp. https://www.datacamp.com/blog/what-is-prompt-engineering-the-future-of-ai-communication

Dai, Y., Liu, A., & Lim, C. P. (2023, April 22). Reconceptualizing ChatGPT and generative AI as a student-driven innovation in higher education. *Procedia CIRP, 119*, 84-90. https://www.sciencedirect.com/science/article/pii/S2212827123004407

DALL·E 2. (2015). Retrieved August 14, 2023, from https://openai.com/dall-e-2

Darcy A, Daniels J, Salinger D, Wicks P, & Robinson A. (2021). Evidence of Human-Level Bonds Established With a Digital Conversational Agent: Cross-sectional, Retrospective Observational Study. *JMIR Formative Research, 5*(5). https://doi.org/10.2196/27868

Darrach, B. (1970). *Meet Shaky, the first electronic person*. Life Magazine, 58–68.

Dean, J. et.al. (2012). *Large scale distributed deep networks*. (F. Pereira and C.J. Burges and L. Bottou and K.Q. Weinberger, Ed.) Advances in Neural Information Processing Systems. . Long Beach, CA.

Devaney, A.J. (1982). A filtered backpropagation algorithm for diffraction tomography. *Ultrasonic Imaging*. 4(4), 226-350. https://www.sciencedirect.com/science/article/abs/pii/0161734682900177

De Vynk, G. (2023, June 28). *ChatGPT maker OpenAI faces a lawsuit over how it used people's data*. Washington Post. https://www.washingtonpost.com/technology/2023/06/28/openai-chatgpt-lawsuit-class-action/

DeGeurin, M. (2023, May 10). *'Thirsty' AI: Training ChatGPT Required Enough Water to Fill a Nuclear Reactor's Cooling Tower, Study Finds*. Gizmodo. 10.https://gizmodo.com/chatgpt-ai-water-185000-gallons-training-nuclear-1850324249

Department of Education Office of Educational Technology. (2023, May). *Artificial Intelligence and the future of teaching and learning*. Insights and Recommendations. Retrieved August 14, 2023, from https://www2.ed.gov/documents/ai-report/ai-report.pdf.

Directorate-General for Research and Innovation. (2024). *Living guidelines on the RESPONSIBLE USE OF GENERATIVE AI IN RESEARCH*. European Commission. https://research-and-innovation.ec.europa.eu/document/2b6cf7e5-36ac-41cb-aab5-0d32050143dc_en

Eaton, L. (2023, January 16). *Classroom policies for AI generative tools* [unpublished manuscript]. College Unbound. Retrieved July 27, 2023, from https://docs.google.com/document/d/1RMVwzjc1o0Mi8Blw_-JUTcXv02b2WRH86vw7mi16W3U/edit

Fass-Holmes, B. (2022). Survey Fatigue-What Is Its Role in Undergraduates' Survey Participation and Response Rates? *Journal of Interdisciplinary Studies in Education*, *11*(1), 56. https://files.eric.ed.gov/fulltext/EJ1344904.pdf

FII Institute (2024) *IMPACT: AI and the Future*. https://fii-institute.org/publication/ai-impact-report-2024/

Finley, T. (2023, March 13). *6 Ways to Use ChatGPT to Save Time*. Edutopia. https://www.edutopia.org/article/6-ways-chatgpt-save-teachers-time/

Fleming, S. (2024, January 15). *Generative artificial intelligence will lead to job cuts this year, CEOs say*. Financial Times. https://www.ft.com/content/908e5465-0bc4-4de5-89cd-8d5349645dda

Fodor, J. & Pylyshyn, Z. (1988). Connectionism and cognitive architecture: A Critical Analysis. *Cognitions 28*(1-2), 2-71. https://www.sciencedirect.com/science/article/abs/pii/0010027788900315

Freire, P. (1970). *Pedagogy of the Oppressed*. The Continuum International Publishing Group Inc.

Gershgorn, D. (2017, Sept 10). *The Quartz guide to artificial intelligence: What is it, why is it important, and should we be afraid?* Quartz. https://qz.com/1046350/the-quartz-guide-to-artificial-intelligence-what-is-it-why-is-it-important-and-should-we-be-afraid

Gibbons, S. (2023, December 7). *How AI Might Impact The Job Market In 2024*. Forbes. https://www.forbes.com/sites/serenitygibbons/2023/12/07/how-ai-might-impact-the-job-market-in-2024

Goodfellow, I., Pouget-Abadie, J., Mirza, M., & Bing, X. (2014). Generative adversarial networks. *Advances in Neural Information Processing Systems 3*(11),139-144. https://arxiv.org/abs/1406.2661

Groumpos, P. (2021). A Critical Historical and Scientific Overview of all Industrial Revolutions. *IFAC-Papers Online*. *54*(13), 464-471. https://doi.org/10.1016/j.ifacol.2021.10.492.

guang-Di, L., Li, Y.-C., Zhang, W., & Zhang, Le. (n.d.). A Brief Review of Artificial Intelligence Applications and Algorithms for Psychiatric Disorders. *Engineering*, 6(4), 462–467. https://www.sciencedirect.com/science/article/pii/S2095809919300657?via%3Dihub

Haan, K. (2023, April 25). *24 Top AI Statistics And Trends In 2024*. Forbes Advisor. https://www.forbes.com/advisor/business/ai-statistics

Hakimshafaei, M. (2023). *Survey of generative AI in architecture and design*. University of California, Santa Cruz. ProQuest Dissertations Publishing.

Hall, M. (2018, April 11). *What is specifications grading and why should you consider using it?* The Innovative Instructor. Retrieved August 4, 2023, from https://ii.library.jhu.edu/2018/04/11/what-is-specifications-grading-and-why-should-you-consider-using-it/

Harvard Online. (2023, April 19). *The benefits and limitations of generative AI.* https://www.harvardonline.harvard.edu/blog/benefits-limitations-generative-ai

Hawley, M. (2023, June 28). *The complete generative AI timeline: History, present and future outlook.* CMSWire. https://www.cmswire.com/digital-experience/generative-ai-timeline-9-decades-of-notable-milestones/

Hicks, M. (2023, August 2). *Scared of AI? Don't be, computer-science instructors say.* The Chronicle of Higher Education. Retrieved August 14, 2023, from https://www.chronicle.com/article/scared-of-ai-dont-be-computer-science-instructors-say

Holloway, J. Cheng, M., & Dickenson, J. (2024, January 13). *Will copyright law enable or inhibit generative AI?* World Economic Forum. Retrieved on March 19, 2024 from https://www.weforum.org/agenda/2024/01/cracking-the-code-generative-ai-and-intellectual-property/

Holmes, W., & Miao, F. (2023). *Guidance for generative AI in education and research.* UNESCO Publishing.

Houhou, K. (2023, December 04). *Revolutionizing Design: The Power of Generative AI.* Parsons. Retrieved on March 19, 2024 from https://www.parsons.com/2023/12/revolutionizing-design-the-power-of-generative-ai/

IBM. (n.d.). *What is an AI model?* IBM. https://www.ibm.com/topics/ai-model

IBM. (2023). *What is artificial intelligence (AI)?* https://www.ibm.com/topics/artificial-intelligence

IBM. (n.d.). *What is deep learning?* Retrieved July 31, 2023, from https://www.ibm.com/topics/deep-learning

IBM. (n.d.). *What is machine learning?* Retrieved July 31, 2023, from https://www.ibm.com/topics/machine-learning

IBM. (n.d.). *What is natural language processing (NLP)?* https://www.ibm.com/topics/natural-language-processing

Infusion. (2023). Multimodality. https://www.sciencedirect.com/topics/computer-science/multimodality#definition

Inspired Learning. (2022). *Examples of Deepfake Technology That Didn't Look Very Fake.* https://inspiredelearning.com/blog/examples-of-deepfake-technology/

Jaiman, A. (2022, August 2). *AI generated synthetic media, aka deepfakes.* Medium. https://towardsdatascience.com/ai-generated-synthetic-media-aka-deepfakes-7c021dea40e1

Jozefowicz, R., Vinyals, O., Schuster, M., Shazeer, N., & Wu, Y. (2016). *Exploring the limits of language modeling.* arXiv.org

Kahn, S. (2023, April). *How AI Could Save (Not Destroy) Education.* TED Talk. https://www.ted.com/talks/sal_khan_how_ai_could_save_not_destroy_education

Kapoor, S. & Narayanan, A. (Jun. 16, 2023) *How to Prepare for the Deluge of Generative AI on Social Media*, Knight First Amend. Inst. Retrieved March 15, 2024, from https://knightcolumbia.org/content/how-to-prepare-for-the-deluge-of-generative-ai-on-social-media

Keller, J., Donoghoe, M., & Perry, A. M. (2024, January 29). *The US must balance climate justice challenges in the era of artificial intelligence.* Brookings Institutions. https://www.brookings.edu/articles/the-us-must-balance-climate-justice-challenges-in-the-era-of-artificial-intelligence/#:~:text=If%20AI%20drives%20more%20resource,toward%20a%20more%20sustainable%20future.

Kelly, J. (2023, March 31). *Goldman Sachs Predicts 300 Million Jobs Will Be Lost Or Degraded By Artificial Intelligence.* Forbes. https://www.forbes.com/sites/jackkelly/2023/03/31/goldman-sachs-predicts-300-million-jobs-will-be-lost-or-degraded-by-artificial-intelligence

Kenyon, A. (2022, September 21). *What is Ungrading?* Duke Learning Innovation. Retrieved August 3, 2023, from https://learninginnovation.duke.edu/blog/2022/09/what-is-ungrading/

Kim, L. (2023, September 12). *AI-Powered 'Thought Decoders' Won't Just Read Your Mind—They'll Change It.* Wired/Ideas. https://www.wired.com/story/ai-thought-decoder-mind-philosophy/

Kjandelwal, K., Patel, S., Patel, J., & Pnachal, M. (2033). A Study to Know – Use of AI for Personalized Recommendation, Streaming Optimization, and Original Content Production at Netflix. *International Journal of Scientific Research & Engineering Trends, 9*(6), 1738–1743. https://ijsret.com/wp-content/uploads/2023/11/IJSRET_V9_issue6_435.pdf

Knight, W. (2022, December 7). ChatGPT's Most Charming Trick Is Also Its Biggest Flaw. Wired. Retrieved September 19, 2023 from https://www.wired.com/story/openai-chatgpts-most-charming-trick-hides-its-biggest-flaw

Kovarik, B. (2016) Second ed. *Revolutions in Communication: Media History from Gutenberg to the Digital Age.* Bloomsbury Academic an imprint of Bloomsbury Publishing.

Krizhevsky, A., Sutskever, H., &Hinton, G. (2012). ImageNet Classification with Deep Convolutional Neural Networks. *Advances in Neural Information Processing System (25).* (NERUIPS Proceedings 2012). F. Pereira, C.J. Burges, L. Bottou and K.Q. Weinberger (eds). Long Beach, CA.

Larson, M. (2023, January 30). *What is contract grading?* Center for Transformative Teaching. Retrieved August 14, 2023, from https://teaching.unl.edu/resources/grading-feedback/contract-grading/#:~:text=Contract%20grading%20is%20a%20type,specific%20grade%20in%20the%20course

Lee, A. (2023, January 26). *What are large language models and why are they important?* NVIDIA Blog. https://blogs.nvidia.com/blog/2023/01/26/what-are-large-language-models-used-for/

Levitt, G. (2000). *The Turk, Chess Automaton.* McFarland & Co.

Liang, W., Yuksekgonul, M., Mao, Y., Wu, E., & Zou, J. (2023, July 10). GPT detectors are biased against non-native English writers. *Patterns, 4*(7), 1-4. https://doi.org/10.1016/j.patter.2023.100779

Lingard, L. (2023). "Writing with ChatGPT: An illustration of its capacity, limitations & implications for academic writers. *Perspectives on Medical Education, 12*(1), 261. https://www.ncbi.nlm.nih.gov/pmc/articles/PMC10312253/

Lium, H., Li, Z., Hall, D., Liagn, P., & Ma, T. (2024). *Sophia: a scalable stochastic second-order optimizer for language model pre-training.* Stanford University, https://arxiv.org/pdf/2305.14342.pdf.

Lock, S. (2022, December 5). What is AI chatbot phenomenon ChatGPT and could it replace humans?. *The Guardian.* https://www.theguardian.com/technology/2022/dec/05/what-is-ai-chatbot-phenomenon-chatgpt-and-could-it-replace-humans

Love, P., Arenas, I. de la T., Learner, S., & Joiner, S. (2024, January 18). *How AI is decoding the animal kingdom.* Financial Times. https://ig.ft.com/ai-animals/

Ludvigsen, K. (2023, March 5). *ChatGPT's Electricity Consumption,* Part II. Medium. https://kaspergroesludvigsen.medium.com/chatgpts-electricity-consumption-pt-ii-225e7e43f22b

Madnick, S. E. (2023). *The Continued Threat to Personal Data: Key Factors Behind the 2023 Increase.* Apple. https://www.apple.com/newsroom/pdfs/The-Continued-Threat-to-Personal-Data-Key-Factors-Behind-the-2023-Increase.pdf

Madnick, S. E. (2024, February 19). *Why Data Breaches Spiked in 2023.* Harvard Business Review. https://hbr.org/2024/02/why-data-breaches-spiked-in-2023

Mair, V. (2023, April 16). *An example of ChatGPT "hallucinating"?* Language Log. https://languagelog.ldc.upenn.edu/nll/?p=58450

Maples, B., Cerit, M., Vishwanath, A., & Pea, R. (2024). Loneliness and suicide mitigation for students using GPT3-enabled chatbots. *Npj Mental Health Research, 3*(1), 4. https://doi.org/10.1038/s44184-023-00047-6

Marcus, G. (2023, August 12). *What if generative AI turned out to be a dud?* Marcus on AI. Retrieved August 14, 2023, from https://garymarcus.substack.com/p/what-if-generative-ai-turned-out

Markoff, J. (2005). Behind artificial intelligence, a squadron of bright real people The New York Times. https://www.nytimes.com/2005/10/14/technology/behind-artificial-intelligence-a-squadron-of-bright-real-people.html

Maroteau, G., An, J., Murgier, J, Hulet, C., Ollivier, M., & Ferreira, A. (2023). Evaluation of the impact of large language learning models on articles submitted to Orthopaedics & Traumatology: Surgery & Research (OTSR): A significant increase in the use of artificial intelligence in 2023. *Orthopaedics & Traumatology, Surgery & Research, 109*(8), 103720. https://doi.org/10.1016/j.otsr.2023.103720

Marr, B. (2023, March 20). *Beyond the Hype: What you Really Need to Know About AI in 2023.* Forbes. https://www.forbes.com/sites/bernardmarr/2023/03/20/beyond-the-hype-what-you-really-need-to-know-about-ai-in-2023/?sh=4ca9b2101315

Martineau, K. (2023, February 15). *What is prompt tuning?* IBM Research Blog. https://research.ibm.com/blog/what-is-ai-prompt-tuning

Martineau, K. (2023, July 24). *What is AI forensics?* IBM Research Blog. https://research.ibm.com/blog/AI-forensics-attribution

McAdoo, T. (2023, April 7). *How to cite ChatGPT.* APA Style. Retrieved August 10, 2023, from https://apastyle.apa.org/blog/how-to-cite-chatgpt

McCulloch, W., & Pitts, W. (1943). A logical calculus of the ideas immanent in nervous activity. *Bulletin of Mathematical Biophysics 5,* 115–133. https://www.cs.cmu.edu/~./epxing/Class/10715/reading/McCulloch.and.Pitts.pdf

McDurmoot, D. (1976). Artificial intelligence meets natural stupidity. *ACM Digital Library, 57*(4-9). https://dl.acm.org/doi/10.1145/1045339.1045340

McMurtrie, B. (2023, May 26). *How ChatGPT could help or hurt students with disabilities.* The Chronicle of Higher Education. Retrieved August 14, 2023, from https://www.chronicle.com/article/how-chatgpt-could-help-or-hurt-students-with-disabilitis

McNeilly, M. & Smith,P. (2023, April 18). *Will Generative AI Disproportionately Affect the Jobs of Women?*, Kenan Institute. UNC Kenan-Flagler Business School. Retrieved March 15, 2024. https://kenaninstitute.unc.edu/kenan-insight/will-generative-ai-disproportionately-affect-the-jobs-of-women/

Messeri, L., & Crockett, M. J. (2024, March). Artificial Intelligence and Illusions of Understanding in Scientific Research. *Nature (687)* 8002,, 49–58, https://doi.org/10.1038/s41586-024-07146-0.

Meta. (2024). *Models and libraries.* Meta. https://ai.meta.com/resources/models-and-libraries/

Metz, C. (2023, November 6). *OpenAI Lets Mom-and-Pop Shops Customize ChatGPT.* The New York Times. https://www.nytimes.com/2023/11/06/technology/openai-custom-chatgpt.html

Metz, C., Chen, B. X., & Weise, K. (2023, September 25). *ChatGPT Can Now Respond With Spoken Words.* The New York Times. https://www.nytimes.com/2023/09/25/technology/chatgpt-talk-digital-assistance.html

Midjourney. (n.d.). Retrieved August 14, 2023, from https://www.midjourney.com/home/?callbackUrl=%2Fapp%2F

Miller, J. (2023, July 27). *Has AI destroyed our critical thinking skills?* Linkedin. https://www.linkedin.com/pulse/has-ai-destroyed-our-critical-thinking-skills-joshua-miller

Minero, E. (2016). *Improving Teaching With Expert Feedback—From Students.* Edutopia.

https://www.edutopia.org/practice/student-surveys-using-student-voice-improve-

Teaching-and-learning

Minsky, M., & Papert, S. (1969). *Perceptrons. An introduction to computational geometry.* The MIT Press LTD.

MLA Style Center. (n.d.). *How do I cite generative AI in MLA style?* Retrieved August 10, 2023, from https://style.mla.org/citing-generative-ai/

Mohan, K. (2023, November 20). *The Intriguing Journey of Constitutional AI in Language Models.* LinkedIn. https://www.linkedin.com/pulse/intriguing-journey-constitutional-ai-language-models-kush-mohan-kjw0c

Mok, A. (2023, May 27). *What is AGI? How artificial general intelligence could make humans obsolete.* Business Insider. https://www.businessinsider.com/what-is-agi-artificial-general-intelligence-explained-2023-5

Moore, G. (1965, April 19). Cramming more components onto integrated circuits. *Electronics, 38*(8), 82-85. . https://www.cs.utexas.edu/~fussell/courses/cs352h/papers/moore.pdf

Munn, L. (2023). The uselessness of AI ethics. *AI and Ethics, 3*(3), 869-877. https://link.springer.com/article/10.1007/s43681-022-00209-w

Mutongoza, B. H., & Olawale, B. E. (2022). Safeguarding Academic Integrity in the Face of Emergency Remote Teaching and Learning in Developing Countries. *Perspectives in Education, 40*(1), 234–249. https://doi.org/10.18820/2519593X/pie.v40.i1.14

NeJame, L., Bharadwaj, R., Shaw, C., & Fox, K. (2023, April 25). *Generative AI in higher education: From fear to experimentation, embracing AI's potential.* Tyton Partners. Retrieved August 14, 2023, from https://tytonpartners.com/generative-ai-in-higher-education-from-fear-to-experimentation-embracing-ais-potential/

Nelson, J. (2023, July 24). *Openai quietly shuts down its ai detection tool.* Decrypt. Retrieved August 10, 2023, from https://decrypt.co/149826/openai-quietly-shutters-its-ai-detection-tool

Newell, A., Shaw, J., & Simon, H. (1959). Report on a general problem-solving program. *Proceedings of the International Conference on Information Processing.* Carnegie Institute of Technology, 256–264. http://bitsavers.informatik.uni-stuttgart.de/pdf/rand/ipl/P-1584_Report_On_A_General_Problem-Solving_Program_Feb59.pdf

Newell, A. & and Simon, H. (1956). *The Logic Theory Machine: A Complex Information Processing System.* The RAND Corporation. http://bitsavers.informatik.uni-stuttgart.de/pdf/rand/ipl/P-1584_Report_On_A_General_Problem-Solving_Program_Feb59.pdf

Nguyen, A., Ngo, H. N., Hong, Y., Dang, B., & Nguyen, B. P. T. (2023). Ethical principles for artificial intelligence in education. *Education and Information Technologies, 28*(4), 4221-4241. https://link.springer.com/article/10.1007/s10639-022-11316-w

NSF, National Science Foundation. (2023, December 14). *Notice to research community: Use of generative artificial intelligence technology in the NSF merit review process.* https://new.nsf.gov/news/notice-to-the-research-community-on-ai

OECD Employment Outlook. (2023) *Artificial Intelligence and the Labour Market.* https://www.oecd.org/employment-outlook/2023/#report

OpenAI. (2024). *Copilot .* Retrieved from

https://copilot.openai.com/

OpenAI. (2023). *ChatGPT (July 2023)*. https://chat.openai.com/chat

Oregon State University Center for Teaching and Learning. (2023). *AI sample syllabus statements and assignment language.* Retrieved July 27, 2023, from

https://ctl.oregonstate.edu/ai-sample-syllabus-statements-and-assignment-language

Pandey, A. (2024). *The AI odyssey from diagnostics to wellness.* PC Quest. https://www.pcquest.com/the-ai-odyssey-from-diagnostics-to-wellness/

Parasuraman R. & Manzey D.H. (2010, June). Complacency and bias in human use of automation: an attentional integration. *Hum Factors, 52*(3), 381-410. doi: 10.1177/0018720810376055.

Partovi, H., & Hongpradit, P. (2024, January 18). *AI and education: Kids need AI guidance in school. But who guides the schools?* World Economic Forum. https://www.weforum.org/agenda/2024/01/ai-guidance-school-responsible-use-in-education/

Peek, S. (2016, March 17). *Knocker uppers: Waking up the workers in industrial Britain.* BBC News. https://www.bbc.com/news/uk-england-35840393

Perlow, J. (2023, December 7). *AI in 2023: A year of breakthroughs that left no human thing unchanged.* ZDNet/Innovation. https://www.zdnet.com/article/generative-ai-will-change-customer-service-forever-heres-how-we-get-there/

Perrigo, B. (2023, December 21). *The 3 Most Important AI Innovations of 2023* . TIME. https://time.com/6547982/3-big-ai-innovations-from-2023/

Personal and Security Research Center. (2022). *Deepfakes and Unintentional Insider Threats* OPA Report No. 2021-087. https://apps.dtic.mil/sti/trecms/pdf/AD1167982.pdf

Piscia, A.I.; Edu, T.; Zaharia, R.M.; & Zaharia, R. (2023). Implementing artificial intelligence in higher education: Pros and cons from the perspectives of academics. *Societies, 13*(118). https://doi.org/10.3390/soc13050118

PM, A. (2023, August 21). *The Top NLP Algorithms to Try and Explore in 2023 for Enhanced Language Understanding.* Analytics Insight. https://www.analyticsinsight.net/top-10-nlp-algorithms-to-try-and-explore-in-2023/

Polyportis, A.& Pahos, N. (2024). Navigating the perils of artificial intelligence: a focused review on ChatGPT and responsible research and innovation. *Humanities and Social Science Communications, 11*(107). https://doi.org/10.1057/s41599-023-02464-6

Popli, N. (2023, April 14). *How to get a six-figure job as an AI prompt engineer.* Time. https://time.com/6272103/ai-prompt-engineer-job/

Prompt engineering. (2023, August 8).*Wikipedia*. https://en.wikipedia.org/wiki/Prompt_engineering

Qualcomm Technologies, Inc. (n.d.). *Q: How do mobile phones use AI? Everything You Need to Know about AI and AI Technology.* https://www.qualcomm.com/products/technology/artificial-intelligence/what-is-ai-faq

Quantum Black, AI by McKinsey. (2023, August 1). *The state of AI in 2023: Generative AI's breakout year.* https://www.mckinsey.com/capabilities/quantumblack/our-insights/the-state-of-ai-in-2023-generative-ais-breakout-year

Radford, A., Wu, J., Rewon, C., Luan, D., Amodei, D., & Sutsjeverm, H. (2018). *Language Models are Unsupervised Multitask Learners.* OpenAI.

Ray, D. (2023, January 30). *How UF developed a model for AI across the curriculum*. University of Florida News. Retrieved August 5, 2023, from https://news.ufl.edu/2023/01/ai-university/

Rhodius, A. (1990). *Apollonius Rhodius: Argonautica*. R C. Seaton (translation) Loeb Classical Library.

Robertson, A. (2024. Feb 21). *Google apologizes for 'missing the mark' after Gemini generated racially diverse Nazis*. The Verge. https://www.theverge.com/2024/2/21/24079371/google-ai-gemini-generative-inaccurate-historical

Rodgers, C. R., & Raider-Roth, M. B. (2002). *Voices Inside Schools. Harvard Educational Review*, 72(2), 230–254. DOI: 10.17763/haer.72.2.5631743606m15751

Rosenblatt, F. (1962). *Principles of Neurodynamics: Perceptrons and the theory of brain mechanisms.* Spartan Books.

Roshanaei, M., Olivares, H., & Lopez, R. R. (2023). Harnessing AI to Foster Equity in Education: Opportunities, Challenges, and Emerging Strategies. *Journal of Intelligent Learning Systems and Applications*, 15(04), 123-143. https://www.scirp.org/journal/paperinformation?paperid=128922

Rumelhart, D., Hinton, G., & Williams, R. (1986). Learning representations by back-propagating errors. *Nature, 323*(6088), 533-536. https://www.cs.toronto.edu/~hinton/absps/naturebp.pdf

Rumelhart, D., , McClelland, J., & PDP Research Group. (1987). *Parallel distribution processing*. MIT Press.

Russell, S., & Norvig, P. (2003). *Artificial Intelligence: A Modern Approach* (2nd ed.). Prentice Hall.

Sag-AFTRA. (2024, January 9). *SAG-AFTRA and Replica Studios Introduce Groundbreaking AI Voice Agreement at CES*. Retrieved on March 19, 2024 from https://www.sagaftra.org/sag-aftra-and-replica-studios-introduce-groundbreaking-ai-voice-agreement-ces

Satariano, A., & Mozur, P. (2023, July). *The People Onscreen Are Fake. The Disinformation Is Real*. New York Times. https://www.nytimes.com/2023/02/07/technology/artificial-intelligence-training-deepfake.html

Schaeffer, R., Miranda, B., & Koyejo, S. (2023). *Are Emergent Abilities of Large Language Models a Mirage?* Proceedings of the 37th Conference on Neural Information Processing Systems. Oh, A., Neumann, T., Globerson, A., Saenko, K., Hardt, M., & Levine, S. (eds). https://openreview.net/pdf?id=ITw9edRDlD

Schmidt, E. (2023, July 5). *This is how AI will transform the way science gets done*. MIT Technology Review. https://www.technologyreview.com/2023/07/05/1075865/eric-schmidt-ai-will-transform-science/

Schweiber, N. & Weiser, B. (2023, June 8). *The Chat GPT Lawyer Explains HImself*. New York Times. https://www.nytimes.com/2023/06/08/nyregion/lawyer-chatgpt-sanctions.html

Seaver, N. (2014). Knowing Algorithms. In *digitalSTS*. Princeton University Press.

Selvi, J. (2022, December 5). *Exploring prompt injection attacks*. NCC Group Research Blog. https://research.nccgroup.com/2022/12/05/exploring-prompt-injection-attacks/

Shaffer, J. (2023, January 11). *Yes, ChatGPT can answer exam questions. But can it write them too?* LinkedIn. https://www.linkedin.com/pulse/yes-chatgpt-can-answer-exam-questions-write-them-too-justin-shaffer/

Shankland, S. (2023, February 19). *Why We're Obsessed with the Mind-Blowing ChatGPT AI Chatbot*. CNET. https://www.cnet.com/tech/computing/why-were-all-obsessed-with-the-mind-blowing-chatgpt-ai-chatbot/

Shapiro, E. (1983). The fifth-generation project — a trip report. *Communications of the ACM. 26* (9), 637–641. https://dl.acm.org/doi/abs/10.1145/358172.358179

Shah, C. (2024). *From Prompt Engineering to Prompt Science With Human in the Loop*. Cornell University, arxiv. https://doi.org/10.48550/ARXIV.2401.04122

Shah, H. (2018). Algorithmic accountability. *Philosophical Transactions of the Royal Society A: Mathematical, Physical and Engineering Sciences, 376*(2128), 1-6. https://royalsocietypublishing.org/doi/epdf/10.1098/rsta.2017.0362

Shieh, J. (2023). *Best practices for prompt engineering with OpenAI API*. OpenAI. https://help.openai.com/en/articles/6654000-best-practices-for-prompt-engineering-with-openai-api

Shonubi, O. (2023, February 21). *AI in the classroom: Pros, cons and the role of ed tech companies*. Forbes. https://www.forbes.com/sites/theyec/2023/02/21/ai-in-the-classroom-pros-cons-and-the-role-of-edtech-companies/amp/

Shulman, K. (2024, January 2). *The creative future of generative AI: An MIT panel charts how artificial intelligence will impact art and design*. MIT News: Arts at MIT. Retrieved March 19, 2024 from https://news.mit.edu/2024/creative-future-generative-ai-0102

Signe, A, Sola-Leyva, A, & Salumets, A. (2023, July). Artificial intelligence in scientific writing: a friend or a foe? *Reproductive BioMedicine Online, 47*(1), 3-9. https://doi.org/10.1016/j.rbmo.2023.04.009.

Singh, R. (2023, August 6). *Asian Student Asks AI For A 'Professional' Pic For LinkedIn, Gets Turned Into…* NDTV World. https://www.ndtv.com/world-news/asian-student-asks-ai-for-a-professional-pic-for-linkedin-gets-turned-into-4274871

Smith, A. (2018).*Public Attitudes Toward Computer Algorithms*. Pew Research Center. https://www.pewresearch.org/internet/2018/11/16/public-attitudes-toward-computer-algorithms/

Søraa, R. (2023, January 27). *AI for diversity*. CRC Press.

Stanford, D. 2023, August 15). *How to Talk to Faculty about AI without Starting World War III*. Retrieved August 17, 2023, from https://danielstanford.substack.com/p/how-to-talk-to-faculty-about-ai-without.

Statista. (2024). U.S. *Undergraduate students' opinions on the use of AI in education 2023*. Retrieved from https://www.statista.com/statistics/1445975/us-undergraduate-students-opinions-on-the-use-of-ai-in-education/

Steen, A. & Lux, M. (2024, February 7). *AI in The Music Industry: Ways AI has Transformed the Business*. Prime Sound. Retrieved on March 19, 2024 from https://primesound.org/ai-in-music/

STL Digital. (2024). *Generative AI in Music Production: A New Era of Sound and Composition*. Retrieved on March 19, 2024 from https://www.stldigital.tech/blog/generative-ai-in-music-production-a-new-era-of-sound-and-composition/

Stupp, C. (2024, January 10). *AI Helps U.S. Intelligence Track Hackers Targeting Critical Infrastructure*. WSJ Pro. https://www.wsj.com/articles/ai-helps-u-s-intelligence-track-hackers-targeting-critical-infrastructure-944553fa

Tang, J., LeBel, A., Jain, S., & Huth, Alexander G. (2023). Semantic reconstruction of continuous language from non-invasive brain recordings. *Nature Neuroscience, 26*, 858–866. https://doi.org/10.1038/s41593-023-01304-9

Tauscher, J. (2020, July 22). *What's the deal with GPT-3?* Medium. https://medium.com/@john.l.tauscher/whats-the-deal-with-gpt-3-78c9d69dfef0

Terra, M., Baklola, M. B., Ali, S., & El-Bastawisy, K. (2023). Opportunities, applications, challenges and ethical implications of artificial intelligence in psychiatry: a narrative review. *The Egyptian Journal of Neurology, Psychiatry and Neurosurgery, 59*(80). https://doi.org/https://doi.org/10.1186/s41983-023-00681-z

Terry, O. (2023, May 12). *I'm a Student. You Have No Idea How Much We're Using ChatGPT*. The Chronicle of Higher Education. https://www.chronicle.com/article/im-a-student-you-have-no-idea-how-much-were-using-chatgpt

Tewari, G. (2022, May 5). *The Future Of AI: 5 Things To Expect In The Next 10 Years*. Forbes. https://www.forbes.com/sites/forbesbusinesscouncil/2022/05/05/the-future-of-ai-5-things-to-expect-in-the-next-10-years

The Authors Guild. (Fall 2023). *The Authors Guild Mobilizes on Multiple Fronts to Protect Writers from AI.*" NY: The Authors Guild Bulletin.

The Authors Guild (2024, February 28). *Ai Best Practices for Authors*. Retrieved March 19, 2024, from https://authorsguild.org/resource/ai-best-practices-for-authors/

Tomko, G & Pendharkar, E. (2023, April 27). *What the Numbers Say About the Drop in School Librarians*. Education Week. https://www.edweek.org/teaching-learning/districts-lost-school-librarians-over-the-pandemic/2023/04

Tregoning, J. (2023). *AI writing tools could hand scientists the "gift of time."* Nature. Retrieved August 1, 2023, from https://doi.org/10.1038/d41586-023-00528-w

Turing, A. (1950). Computing Machinery and Intelligence. *Mind*, 49, 433-460.

United Nations Educational, Scientific and Cultural Organization. (2022). *Recommendation on the Ethics of Artificial Intelligence*. Retrieved September 19, 2023, from https://unesdoc.unesco.org/in/documentViewer.xhtml?v=2.1.196&id=p::usmarcdef_0000381137&file=/in/rest/annotationSVC/DownloadWatermarkedAttachment/attach_import_e86c4b5d-5af9-4e15-be60-82f1a09956fd%3F_%3D381137eng.pdf&locale=en&multi=true&ark=/ark:/48223/pf0000381137/PDF/381137eng.pdf#1517_21_EN_SHS_int.indd%3A.8962%3A15

University of Sydney. (n.d.) *AI in education*. Retrieved August 5, 2023, from https://canvas.sydney.edu.au/courses/51655

Utah Tech University. (2023). *Generative AI tools: Guidelines for teaching and learning*. Retrieved August 3, 2023, from https://ctl.utahtech.edu/aitools/

Valtolina, S., & Hu, L. (2021). *Charlie: A chatbot to improve the elderly quality of life and to make them more active to fight their sense of loneliness*. 14th Biannual Conference of the Italian SIGCHI Chapter, Article No. 19, 1–5. https://doi.org/10.1145/3464385.3464726

Van Cleave, K., & Novak, A. (2023, November 27). *Amazon is using AI to deliver packages faster than ever this holiday season*. CBS Mornings. https://www.cbsnews.com/news/amazon-faster-deliveries-ai-holiday-season-cyber-monday-deals/

Varanasi, L. (2023, November 5). *GPT-4 can ace the bar, but it only has a decent chance of passing the CFA exams. Here's a list of difficult exams the ChatGPT and GPT-4 have passed*. Business Insider. https://www.businessinsider.com/list-here-are-the-exams-chatgpt-has-passed-so-far-2023-1

Verma, P. (2023, May 19). *A professor accused his class of using ChatGPT, putting diplomas in jeopardy*. Washington Post. Retrieved August 12, 2023, from https://www.washingtonpost.com/technology/2023/05/18/texas-professor-threatened-fail-class-chatgpt-cheating/

Villarroel, V., Bloxham, S., Bruna, D., Bruna, C., & Herrera-Seda, C. (2018). Authentic assessment: Creating a blueprint for course design. *Assessment & Evaluation in Higher Education*, 43(5), 840–854. https://doi.org/10.1080/02602938.2017.1412396.

Vicente, L., & Matute, H. (2023). Humans inherit artificial intelligence biases. *Scientific reports*, 13, https://www.nature.com/articles/s41598-023-42384-8#citeas

Vincent, J. (2018, April 17). *Watch Jordan Peele use AI to make Barack Obama deliver a PSA about fake news*. The Verge. https://www.theverge.com/tldr/2018/4/17/17247334/ai-fake-news-video-barack-obama-jordan-peele-buzzfeed

Vyas. DA., Jones, DS., Meadows, AR., Diouf, K., Nour, NM., & Schantz-Dunn, J. (2019). Challenging the Use of Race in the Vaginal Birth after Cesarean Section Calculator. *Women's Health Issues, 29*(3), 201-204. https://pubmed.ncbi.nlm.nih.gov/31072754/.

Walter, Y. (2024). Embracing the future of Artificial Intelligence in the classroom: the relevance of AI literacy, prompt engineering, and critical thinking in modern education. *International Journal of Educational Technology in Higher Education, 21*(1), 15-. https://doi.org/10.1186/s41239-024-00448-3

Weise, K. & Metz, C. ((2023, May 1). *When AI chatbots hallucinate*. The New York Times. Retrieved August 5, 2023, from https://www.nytimes.com/2023/05/01/business/ai-chatbots-hallucination.html#:~:text=And%20sometimes%20the%20chatbots%20make,could%20ever%20analyze%2C%20even%20A.I.

Weywadt, C., Schneider, K., Guiffre, M., Ellis, S., & Jaros, S. *Deepfakes and Unintentional Insider Threats*. Pew Research Center, OPA Report No. 2021-087. https://apps.dtic.mil/sti/trecms/pdf/AD1167982.pdf

Whitehead, A. & Russell, B. (1910). *Principia Mathematica*. Vol. 1 (1st ed.).Cambridge University Press.

Wiggers, K. (2023, Nov 6). As OpenAI's multimodal API launches broadly, research shows it's still flawed. *TechCrunch*. https://techcrunch.com/2023/11/06/openai-gpt-4-with-vision-release-research-flaws/

Williams, M. (1997). *A History of Computing Technology,* 2nd ed. IEEE Computer Society Press.

Willige, A. (2023, October 31). How AI can speed scientific discovery, from predicting virus variants to vital protein research. *World Economic Forum*. https://www.weforum.org/agenda/2023/10/ai-for-good-science-discovery/

Wilson, B., Hoffman, J. & Morgenstern, J. (2019). Predictive Inequality in Object Detection. *arXiv*, https://arxiv.org/pdf/1902.11097.pdf

Woebot Health. (2024). *Relational Agent for Mental Health. Behavioral Health, at Scale.* https://woebothealth.com/

World Economic Forum. (2023). *Future of Jobs Report 2023: Up to a Quarter of Jobs Expected to Change in Next Five Years*. https://www.weforum.org/press/2023/04/future-of-jobs-report-2023-up-to-a-quarter-of-jobs-expected-to-change-in-next-five-years/

Writers Guild of America. (2023). *WGA Contract 2023 Summary of the 2023 WGA MBA*. Retrieved March 19, 2024 from https://www.wgacontract2023.org/the-campaign/summary-of-the-2023-wga-mba

Wood, Gaby (2003). *Living Dolls: A Magical History of the Quest for Mechanical Life*. Faber.

Wu, C. (2024). Past Imperfect: How credit scores "bake in" and perpetuate past discrimination. *Racial Justice and Equal Economic Opportunity, National Consumer Law Center*. https://www.nclc.org/wp-content/uploads/2016/05/20240227_Issue-Brief_Past-Imperfect.pdf

Xames, M., & Shefa, J. (2023, April 1). ChatGPT for Research and Publication: Opportunities and Challenges. *Journal of Applied Learning & Teaching, 6*(1).https://doi.org/10.37074/jalt.2023.6.1.20.

Yang, W., shao, Y., & Xu, Y.. (2023). Guidelines on clinical research evaluation of artificial intelligence in ophthalmology. *International Journal of Ophthalmology, 16*(9), 1361–1372. https://doi.org/10.18240/ijo.2023.09.02

Young, J.R. (2023, July 27). Instructors rush to do 'assignment makeovers' to respond to ChatGPT. Edsurge. Retrieved August 14, 2023, from https://www.edsurge.com/news/2023-07-27-instructors-rush-to-do-assignment-makeovers-to-respond-to-chatgpt

Zakir, M. H., Khan, S. H., Saeed, Z., & Sajida. (2023). The Impact of Artificial Intelligence on Intellectual Property Rights. *INTERNATIONAL JOURNAL of HUMAN and SOCIETY*, 3(4), 312–319. https://ijhs.com.pk/index.php/IJHS/article/view/330

Zeide, E. (2019, August 26). *Artificial Intelligence in Higher Education: Applications, Promise and Perils, and Ethical Questions*. Educause. https://er.educause.edu/articles/2019/8/artificial-intelligence-in-higher-education-applications-promise-and-perils-and-ethical-questions

Zwass, V. (2023, July 19). *Neural network*. Britannica. https://www.britannica.com/technology/neural-network